Managing a Sales Team

And Succeeding

Tom Butler

Published by Business Skills Press LLC
P. O. Box 690656
Vero Beach, Florida 32969

ISBN 978-0-9772169-2-5
Library of Congress Control Number 2007902526

Printed and bound in the United States of America
by Sheridan Books, Inc.
Ann Arbor, Michigan 48103

Cover Design, Artwork & Layout by Artline Graphics, Sedona, AZ
Manuscript Assistant Margo Gravesen
Edited by Mary Ranjana Blackett
Web Design & Hosting by AzureFire LLC, Las Vegas, NV
Photographs and illustrations © istockphoto.com and © dreamstime.com

Dedication

To those whose presence and memory reminds me
the celebration of family
is the most precious of all gatherings.

Anna and John, Don and Martha, Linda, Patti...
Charlie and Margaret...
Kristen, Timothy, Meghan and Margo.

Table of Contents

Introduction

PART I
Sales Managers Must Lead!

Chapter 1   11
Leadership Begins With Communication!

Chapter 2   31
Goals Are Paramount

Chapter 3   39
Motivating A Team

Chapter 4   47
Coaching Performance And Achievement

Chapter 5   55
Control The Selling Environment

Chapter 6   69
Manage The Metrics

Chapter 7   75
Hold Them Accountable For Results...Every Day!

Chapter 8   81
Account Management

Chapter 9   91
Effective Forecasting

Chapter 10   123
The Management And Creation Of Budgets

Chapter 11   133
Evaluating Salespeople

Chapter 12   159
Sales Compensation Plans

Chapter 13   171
Powerful Sales Meetings

Chapter 14   181
All Sales Managers Have Four Constituencies

Table of Contents

PART II
Sales Management Assignments

Chapter 15   189
The Transition To Sales Management
Chapter 16   195
Succeeding In Your First Assignment
Chapter 17   205
Sales Managers Without Sales Experience

PART III
The Truth About Managing

Chapter 18   213
Salespeople Are—Salespeople!
Chapter 19   217
What's Your Personal Contribution?
Chapter 20   221
The Assignment Is Temporary...The Results Aren't!
Chapter 21   225
Failure—Why It Happens

Appendix A   236
Appendix B   237
Appendix C   238
Index   242
About The Author   246

Introduction

In my career, I've enjoyed a number of significant managerial assignments. In hindsight, the time I spent managing sales teams was by far the most rewarding and challenging of experiences.

Businesses ultimately succeed or fail in a direct relationship to the achievements of the sales teams they send into competitive markets. The all-important suspects, prospects and customers are engaged and won or lost each and every business day. At the most fundamental of levels, sales teams and their managers come to understand the strengths and failings of every product, service and business plan that their organizations present to their markets.

Managing a sales team is in many ways a unique experience because the results of your efforts, leadership, and decision making are laid bare. The team either makes its revenue target, or fails to achieve plan! Black and white performance criteria present little wiggle room for explanation or spin.

Sales practitioners by their nature are both a pleasure and demanding to manage. They enter sales with diverse goals, personalities and expectations; but they all have a need for, and a right to expect, competent leadership and management. When the management they experience falters or underperforms, the results they deliver suffer...and it quickly shows at many levels. Managing a selling team is not an assignment for the timid, indecisive or faint of heart.

Why choose to be a sales manager? The rewards. You will discover you can make a true difference in the lives of the people entrusted to your care, to your customers and prospects. It's fulfilling to deliver products or services that change the fortunes of your clients, to help solve real business problems and advance careers. Knowing your efforts can have a significant impact on the business where you work is also rewarding.

I have written *Managing a Sales Team And Succeeding* because I believe the very best sales managers are those who focus on helping their salespeople achieve the most significant professional standing they are capable of reaching. They bring the same attitude to assisting their customers, prospects and business. The success their teams achieve is the reward they experience for their leadership. "What's in it for me?" is subjugated to "When I make others successful, then I achieve success!" We will show you how to embrace this managerial philosophy and why it will set your

7

performance apart from other managers.

Deciding to be a sales manager may be imminent or years in your future. Preparing for this complex opportunity can never start too soon. Exploring the challenge ahead is part of expanding your business experience, life skills and career plan. Perhaps you are already a sales manager, one who needs to get proficient in your assignment...quickly! This book will get you up to speed.

Part I—Sales Managers Must Lead will give you a comprehensive understanding of the skills, disciplines and strategies the top sales managers understand, accept and trust. The topics start at a fundamental skill level and advance in complexity.

Integrated in the text are case studies that follow the experience of several new sales managers as they grow in experience and stature. You will come to know Robert, Karen and Norton, as well as their VP of Sales, Al Winters. The company they work for, Baker Industries, and the characters themselves are all fictionalized.

The dialogue reinforces the learning points in each chapter and gives the reader a feel for real-life conversations and challenges faced by sales managers each business day—the same conversations you will personally experience in your career's journey!

Part II—The range of **Sales Management Assignments** and challenges you will be asked to undertake is explained in this section. The transition to sales management can be a difficult journey because it is so different from the role assigned to individual sales contributors. We will help prepare you for the experience and get you off to a fast start.

Part III—The Truth About Managing gives you insights that come from years of practical experience in managing salespeople. The awareness you gain will help you lead a sales team and avoid predictable mistakes. Our discussion lays bare five common points of failure and why a focus on personal contribution is so important for new managers.

In truth, sales management is a very difficult assignment, which is why the career rewards for performing well are extraordinary—both immediately and in the future!

PART I

SALES MANAGERS MUST LEAD!

CHAPTER 1

Leadership Begins With Communication!

The first day you spend as a Sales Manager is a watershed career event. Your performance will now be judged by the achievement of the members of your selling team. They alone will ultimately reflect your competence and contributions as a leader. You cannot and will not succeed if they fail to perform!

Unlike so many other managerial assignments, the criteria for judging success are quite clear and public. Did your sales team achieve its plan, quota, revenue target or whatever term is applicable? Make plan and you may well be judged as a successful sales manager, fail to reach your goal and sooner or later your assignment will end with a harsh verdict.

Learning to become a successful sales manager is the start of a journey from individual contribution to managerial accountability and leadership. It is how many business people get their first experience managing a highly visible company revenue assignment, which can lead to ever increasing amounts of responsibility and career opportunities. It is also where many entrepreneurs confront the very real challenge of running a successful business venture and serving as leaders.

The first fundamental skill every sales leader must learn to master is how to communicate! I like to remind readers that communicating with other people is really simple. We all have communicated countless thoughts, ideas, moments of happiness and occasional anger since childhood. We each have spoken with and listened to countless individuals. The difficult part of communicating is doing it well!

I want to illustrate my point by telling you the story of several new sales managers who are embarking on a journey many of you will or have already begun...

Why Do Communication Skills Matter?

The rumors had circulated for months—several new sales managers were going to be appointed. The current salesforce agreed on very little, but they were unanimous in their concern about how the new managers would impact the organization. They understood a leadership change was afoot; some of them openly welcomed a new regime, while others were angry and quite concerned. Arguments ranged from big picture discussions to the mundane and personal. Will this policy change? Suppose the new manager wants to...assign new territories, change compensation plans or bring in a new team? When the announcement was finally made, everyone focused his or her attention on the new managers and the introductory meetings which were about to occur.

Robert had finally become a director of sales. It seemed like the wait had been much too long, many of his friends had already been promoted to management positions, but more than anything else he felt competitively relieved his time had arrived. He had been so focused on getting this assignment that he had, in fact, spent very little time thinking beyond his own promotion. How he would manage the team he was about to inherit just had not been a priority.

Not particularly gifted as a speaker, he experienced nervousness as he was introduced to a crowded room. His mind raced...as reality began to dawn like an approaching freight train! An adrenaline rush was telling his brain...you...are in a world of trouble! A lot of sharp penetrating eyes were sizing him up and making judgments. Someone handed him a microphone. Dry-throated and thick-tongued he tried to speak.

"Hi...my name is Robert. I am looking forward to my new assignment. I have been in sales for over three years at..."

The audience was dead silent; its first impression best summed up by two senior sales representatives in the back of the room, "Just another rookie delivered to an assignment he can't possibly succeed at; ignore him and in time he'll disappear." They got up and left the room. Their selling time was too important to waste on this meeting.

In the third row, an older sales executive whispered to a young friend, "There are two types of sales managers—those who grow people and organizations and those who fail people and damage businesses."

Karen had finally become a director of sales. A decade as a top sales performer had given her the opportunity to observe a gamut of sales managers. Karen had worked for the good, the bad and the true disasters. She had carefully prepared herself for this promotion. In fact, she had delayed accepting a management assignment for several years, just to be certain it was truly what she wanted. 'If I do this, I intend to be very good...and very successful! It's about helping each person on this team get better and achieve their own goals for success.'

As she was introduced, the butterflies began. Her mind refocused, 'Work your plan, you are only going to get one chance to set the agenda for this team and make a strong first impression.'

"Good morning! I've spent the last several weeks looking at the performance of this sales team and each of your backgrounds. I am certain we all agree on two facts...First, there is an enormous amount of talent in this room. Second, this team is ready to begin to perform well beyond what it has delivered in the last three years. I took this assignment because I believe I can help each of you to become better sales executives. My job is to get you what you need in order to reach your own personal goals as professionals. No one is more aware than I am of this simple reality...my personal success will come from your achieving success!" She paused and looked into the audience, "Where is Bob Kelly?"

He quickly raised his hand.

"Bob, I understand you were the top sales representative for the last two years?"

"Yes, I am...was!"

"Do you believe you can do better?"

"Yes, I do..."

"What can I do, right now, to help you sell more product?"

"I need more time on the road and less meetings here at the office."

"Where is Tad Smith? Who is Stephen McWilson?"

The audience was buzzing and fully engaged. Another pause, this time Karen set her initial agenda.

"I am going to meet with each of you this week. I want to hear your suggestions and ideas on how we get organized and improve our selling performance and how you're going to improve your personal results. We are also going to agree on what we specifically expect you to achieve in the next 90 days. I told you what my job is. Now, I want to talk about what I expect from each of you!"

The audience gave a collective laugh and its acknowledgement.

"Good...you knew I wasn't the only person who gets to make commitments and is held accountable. Salespeople get paid to sell. It's why you all chose this profession and are here. I expect your best efforts, your full attention and real commitment! And I expect you to deliver results! Speaking of results and to honor my commitment to Bob Kelly, our meeting time is over, it's time for you to get back to selling! I look forward to working with each of you, learning and building a team that will be a wonderfully successful career experience for each of us!"

Bob Kelly and Tad Smith knew change was in the air and a new leader had arrived. In the third row, the mature gentleman smiled and uttered but one word to his young apprentice... "Gardener."

What did Karen know that Robert didn't? She understood that the first fundamental skill all successful sales managers master is communications.

14

Fundamental Communications Skills

- Think before you speak
- Learn to listen
- Ask questions to learn
- Speak the language of your audience
- Say what you mean...mean what you say
- Keep repeating the message...until they listen!
- Speak with candor
- Clear, concise and personalized speech
- Engage each audience!

Think before you speak

How many times have you wished you could take back something you said? A statement which was harsh, inaccurate, hurtful or just plain stupid! Unfortunately, as humans, the vast majority of us come in time to learn...once you have said something, it does not easily go away. In fact, it often has a way of coming back to undermine your future efforts at the most inopportune times.

Being reminded that your current position on an important policy issue is inconsistent with what you said yesterday or last week is uncomfortable at best. If these occurrences become frequent events, your credibility and leadership are called into question. People don't like to work for or with managers who are inconsistent about their goals and objectives.

Effective sales managers learn that communicating with an audience is much too important to be left to random pronouncements, poorly reasoned statements or meaningless conversations. The audience may be your sales team, your customers, business partners or a single individual.

I resigned my first sales position...when in a moment of profound anger, my sales manager expressed how he personally disliked anyone and everyone in sales! I had worked too hard and achieved too much professional success to spend my time working for someone who clearly had a prejudicial opinion of me, and my colleagues! His subsequent denials, apologies and offers of special concessions did not change the reality of his words. I sincerely believed he regretted his comments, but the bond of trust and respect between us was damaged beyond repair.

Leaders are held to a higher standard. They understand the importance of thinking before they speak. Does this mean they must always script their conversations? No, but I do believe they must embrace a conscious thought process, recognizing how important it is to communicate messages that support the goals they seek to achieve.

It is difficult to communicate effectively; it is almost impossible to succeed when you are just shooting from the hip or thinking out loud. Effective communication skills start with deciding on a GOAL, taking ACTION to achieve your goal and measuring the RESULTS of your discussion or message.

Leaders understand that what you say—and how you say it—is too important to be left to chance. If it is important enough to be communicated, it is important enough to be well-thought out and carefully constructed.

Learn to listen
One of the oddities of human nature is we all want to be heard. Unfortunately, many of us don't want to be the person who gets to listen. In truth, learning to listen can be a difficult skill to master, but the dividends it pays are enormous and immediate.

Why is it difficult to listen? It requires one to focus on the other person, and to put their needs and desires ahead of your own. When we listen, we expose ourselves to what someone else thinks, believes and values. Often their thoughts and opinions are difficult to swallow because they are different from our own. Listening means you get to hear things that can be unpleasant or difficult to accept. Sometimes listening means you hear direct criticism of yourself, your own ideals and facts you hold dear!

When you expose yourself to listening, a curious thing happens. People begin to tell you more of what they think, and often behave with both candor and honesty. They find comfort in knowing you will listen, even if you are not always in agreement. Trust and respect begin to build.

Listening starts when you focus on the other person, make and hold eye contact with them and approach each conversation with a sincere sense of openness. *"Tell me what's on your mind. I am going to listen, ask questions and learn from our conversation. I am not going to pass judgment on what we discuss. We may or may not agree, but it is important for the both of us to express and share our views."*

Managers must also consciously seek out a diverse audience. Restricting your conversations to team members with whom you are comfortable or only those who are your best sales performers, limits your exposure to the pulse of your full team.

Listening can be especially difficult for those managers and personalities who are accustomed to being in control. It is easier to be told exactly what you want to hear, when you want to hear it, on your own terms! It is also a path to isolation from your team and eventually to poor decision making. A keen understanding of reality can come from effective listening.

Robert was struggling with his team's poor performance. The executives upstairs were beginning to express concern about another weak month of sales results.

"Look, I am not happy about the numbers you are delivering!" Tad Smith knew this drill all too well. He was the tenth salesperson Robert had called on the carpet this week.

"Actually, my forecast for the next several months looks solid. I will be just fine by year end."

"Well, that's news to me!"

Smitty began to simmer. He rarely saw Robert. He had solicited one quick 'good morning' weeks ago. Nothing had changed since Robert arrived. Apparently, frequent communications with his sales team was not a priority. It was not clear to anyone on the team just what he did. "My desk is right outside your office and I am more than willing to update you on my accounts whenever you would like."

"Why haven't you come to me and asked for a meeting?"

"Well, let's just say your door has not been exactly open."

"That's your problem, Mr. Smith...make an appointment!"

"Are you kidding me?"

"What's that supposed to mean?"

"It's supposed to mean that I have sold for this company for over twenty years, made my plan and more every year, brought dozens of new customers to the business...and in three months, you have never asked for my advice, invited me to get a cup of coffee or even gone out of your way to acknowledge my presence. That's what it means!" Smitty's face was crimson and his demeanor was confrontational. He pushed his chair back and left Robert's office. He was headed straight upstairs to see his old boss. Enough is enough!

Karen was also struggling with her team's poor performance.

"I need to assure executive management that our sales results, though disappointing, are on track; how do you suggest we do that?"

The entire sales team had shown up for her Saturday morning meeting, those who were not physically present were on a teleconference line.

"Management has a right to be concerned with our performance and ask questions...I want to be sure we give them an accurate response supported by facts."

Steve McWilson went to the whiteboard and started to graph some numbers. "Karen, you need to know we go through this drill every year, the last 60 days have been historically weak sales months. Our prospects go on vacation in July and August, an inconvenient truth."

McWilson continued, "We should have done some special incentives, but the Vice President of Sales stopped those last year. Here's the good news, sales are up 6% over last year same period, and 8% over the year before."

Bob Kelly counselled her, "Just remind them of those numbers and present the forecast for the rest of the year which really looks good. Don't over-promise, but let them know that you and the salespeople are confident."

Someone else suggested, "May be a good opportunity for you to suggest a year-end sales promotion to make it clear you want to leave nothing on the table."

Everyone wanted to voice a suggestion!

"I would remind them you have three major orders waiting on the delivery of the SC6000 units. Get those systems certified, and we'll get a real nice revenue bump!"

Karen listened attentively, took careful notes of each suggestion and asked lots of questions. Their advice was important information. She thanked her team for giving up a Saturday morning and knew she would spend the rest of the day analyzing this mass of material.

On the way to the parking lot, Kelly volunteered, "I'm going to see our CEO at a charity event this evening, I will make a point of telling him how optimistic we all are about the progress you're making and that our sales are following a normal trendline. Are you okay with that?"

"Thanks, Bob. I appreciate your help and advice! See you Monday at the airport."

"Hey boss, I'll call you Sunday evening to go over the plan for Monday's call!"

"Okay, that's fine. I'd also like to run my presentation to management past you."

Learn to listen!

Ask questions to learn

When you learn to listen you will discover that asking questions comes easily. It's an extension of listening. Asking questions is critical to effective sales management for a simple reason...you need to learn and understand the internal and external realities that impact your team's performance. Leaders can't point the way forward if they are both blind to and ignorant of their environment!

Learning comes from asking open-ended questions: Who? What? When? Where? Why? and How? Listen carefully to the answers with a non-judgmental attitude and manner. You will discover some people welcome questions and sharing information, while others struggle with the exchanges.

Team members who are uncomfortable answering questions need to be assured of your intention. "I can't do my best if I don't understand what's going on. I know you are a professional and I value your input and opinions. This is how I deal with everybody on the sales team."

In truth, it will take some personalities longer periods of time and more assurances to get comfortable sharing ideas and information with you or anyone else. Salespeople who have worked in environments which discourage much communication can be wary. Respect the confidence of your sales staff by being discreet with their conversations and don't use the conversations to discipline or criticize anybody.

Asking questions means you also have to be prepared to answer questions. Telling your team the answers flow only in one direction is foolish and counterproductive. Responding requires candor, honesty and occasionally telling the other party, "I don't know the answer to your question," or, "I can't answer your question." Remember our discussion about thinking before you speak!

The more questions you ask and respond to, the more communications within your team will flourish. Your team will quickly judge if you are using the communication process to create positive momentum. If they decide your intentions are misguided or counterproductive, the communications channels will close down very quickly. You certainly don't want salespeople sitting in front of you thinking, 'The last two people who answered that question got fired!'

One of the many benefits of asking questions to learn is the amount of information, knowledge, opinions and suggestions you will quickly discover. The exposure can be the difference between a rapid learning curve and a long protracted introduction to your new assignment. In sales management, quick studies are always valuable and preferred.

Speak the language of your audience

Communication is difficult enough without stumbling over different vocabularies and business terminologies. Learn all the current terms and definitions used within your business and the external marketplace as quickly as possible. Why? You want to eliminate as much confusion and as many misunderstandings as possible. I found it was often easiest initially to adopt the current vocabulary of the sales team. In time, you can introduce the terms and nomenclature you prefer.

How do I learn what the vocabulary in use encompasses? Listen and ask questions, then expect early on to get an occasional surprise!

Robert's first sales meeting agenda required every salesperson to bring their current pipeline. Sitting in the conference room he listened to the first presenter.

"So...what are you going to close this month? I don't see that on the pipeline."

"It's not on my pipeline."

"Well, where is it?"

"That would be on my forecast."

"Okay...let's go through the forecast."

"I'm sorry, Robert, but I didn't bring a forecast. Your message said we were discussing pipeline which is all I brought."

"Pipelines include forecasts!"

The heads around the table were all shaking...no!

"Pipelines include forecasts!"

Joel spoke up, "Not in our world they don't!"

Robert shook off his confusion and realized he needed to explore a laundry list of sales terms with his new team.

Karen and Bob Kelly were finishing a contract negotiation session with an important customer. The CFO asked Karen a simple question, "Can I assume you will accept our note as payment for the merchandise? May I have your assurance the paper will not be resold to a commercial factoring house?"

Karen was speechless and it showed.

Bob quickly stepped in and answered the question, "Karen is not familiar with our financing arrangements. We've asked her to learn so much in the last month about our business and products, this issue has slipped through the cracks. Let me explain what we are willing to offer."

Say what you mean...mean what you say!
The value of consistency in your communications is important. Your team will observe if you live by what you communicate.

I always chuckle when I recall a former manager who constantly made a point of lecturing the sales team about managing travel costs. No one was ever to fly first class, except him or anyone else he decided to exempt often on a whim! When I booked him a room in a budget hotel, he was quite unhappy. The message was clear, he had no real interest in managing travel costs.

Communicate enough empty or contradictory messages and your team begins to view your leadership as hypocrisy or worse. If you promise something, be prepared to deliver on the promise whether it be good, bad or indifferent. Demonstrating to your team you really don't mean what you say puts them in a logical position to suspect anything and everything you communicate. Employees who are forced to ask, "How can I judge whether he or she really means what they have said?" quickly cripple any organization. The importance of learning to think before you speak reverberates through this discussion because you may be judged on and forced to act upon your pronouncements regardless of their wisdom.

Robert was angry at the messenger sitting in his office. The Comptroller of his division held a memorandum in his hand. "It says you will terminate anyone who fails to file their expense reports within 60 days of the actual date of travel."

"Yeah!"

"Well, I have six salespeople who have violated the policy you chose to establish!"

"How many?"

"Six! Which is one quarter of your present team!"

"I'm not going to fire six salespeople!"

"I understand that..." He walked to the office door and closed it. "Robert, I know this is your first sales management job; but you are making a lot of mistakes and your boss is starting to notice. Here's some free advice. Before you issue any more policy statements, ask for some help. Let somebody review this stuff, so you don't get caught in an embarrassing situation."

"Okay."

"I am going to ignore the memo for another week. Figure out how to fix the problem or rescind your policy."

"How can I rescind the policy?"

"You don't have much choice. Unfortunately, whatever you do will damage your standing with the sales team."

The Comptroller's next stop was Karen's office. "We have to talk about late expense reports."

Karen peered over her glasses and motioned him to sit down.

"Have you set a policy yet?"

"No, I just haven't had time."

"I just had to tell Robert he can't fire one quarter of his salesforce over a violation of his policy."

Karen giggled, "Nothing personal, but I don't fire salespeople who are late with their expense forms. I can't understand why someone will not take fifteen minutes to fill one out, but termination is definitely not the solution."

"Can I suggest a policy?"

"I would certainly appreciate your help. In fact, why don't you write it up and we can get together and review it."

"Do you want the tough version or leniency?"

"I want the fair version that I can support and enforce without any hesitation."

Keep repeating the message...until they listen!

It never ceases to amaze me how often some messages have to be repeated. Experienced managers appreciate that not all of their followers are good listeners. I also suspect the ever-present skeptics insist on hearing a message several times before they acknowledge it's real and that you are serious about its communication.

Don't assume your team gets your message until their actions support it or they begin to tell you...*Okay, we get it!* Even then, I suggest you communicate it yet again to reinforce how serious and important the message really is. I learned as a CEO that if I didn't talk about our company's key goals at every company meeting, someone would inevitably question, after the meeting, if we had goals and what they were!

What happens if the team objects to my message or continues to question it? I can assure you they will! Don't be surprised that some messages will be fought and others ignored as long as possible. A message of change can cause real resistance, as can communications which impact the 'sacred cows' every business has adopted.

The way to deal with this behavior is no different than basic sales objection handling. Determine what all the objections are, and explain your position on each. Resolve the key objections first and then deal with the minor concerns. Don't be drawn into the emotional frenzy which can arise. Speak calmly and listen carefully. The audience may not agree with your position; in the end, they may grudgingly accept your message. Keep repeating it until they listen.

The room was in a state of commotion. Karen had suspected this was going to be a tough sell, but it was turning out to be even worse than expected. Two memos, several e-mails and a previous meeting seemed to have mattered very little.

"You're telling us we are getting compact cars next year?"

"Giving up our full size SUVs?"

"No way, Karen!"

"Whose brainstorm was this?"

"Talk about cutting benefits!"

"Okay, okay! Please, everybody just listen for a moment. I know you're less than pleased and change is difficult to accept at times. Our owners have mandated a 10% cost reduction for every department—no exceptions. We can reduce staff, cut commission plans, restrict travel...or, switch to less costly automobiles."

"They may not be safe!"

"We haven't selected a model yet and safety will be a prime consideration. We'll reach our 10% cost reduction from nothing more than the savings due to increased gas mileage. I believe it's the best way to solve the budget issue with a minimal amount of pain. The alternatives are much worse!"

"Are you going to drive a compact?"

"No, I'm not. I gave up my company car and will be riding the bus to work, then walking three blocks to the office."

The grumbling subsided and someone commented, "I'm still not sure they will be safe!"

"I believe they will be safe. However, you can opt to drive your own personal car and the company will reimburse you at 25 cents per mile."

Karen knew this argument would not die easily, but the facts were on the table and would eventually be accepted.

Speak with candor

The most powerful messages are communicated with passion and candor. Listeners respond because they know the speaker believes in the message. They may accept or reject some or all of your presentation but you will be respected for candor and passion.

Audiences also know when they are being patronized and misled. It may take several communications, but as they observe and come to know the speaker, their judgments crystallize. Double-speak, evasiveness and babbling are the anthesis of passion and candor. The damages these qualities can cause a leader are substantial and often cannot be reversed: "Why did he (or she) attempt to mislead us?"..."She is being evasive!"..."How come you didn't just tell us the facts?"

Sometimes, it is very difficult to speak with passion and candor. Sales managers understand that they are occasionally asked to deliver messages for which they do not have much enthusiasm.

I worked for a very difficult CEO, who had a great number of strengths, but also several glaring weaknesses. There was little input, discussion or consultative decision making. She insisted that any bad news or difficult decisions be presented by someone else and be completely disassociated from her. The messenger would then be blamed for any fallout from her personal decisions. This was what 'team players' did in her organization. Comically, very few of the company's employees were unaware of her tactics.

I decided to speak with candor even if I could not find passion for her decisions. I delivered her messages, listened to the often justifiable complaints, explained the decisions as best I could and then implemented them.

I was often chided, "You thought of this all by yourself?" My answer was always the same..."I must have!"

My refusal to protect her from taking responsibility for her own singular decision making was a constant source of friction in our relationship. My approach, though controversial, allowed our sales team to grow personal bonds of respect and trust which were so important to our collective achievement, even under difficult circumstances.

Your sales team must, at the very least, know you are honestly and candidly sharing important news with them. Why? You want them to learn and act on this information because you value and respect their full participation. Communications driven by genuine passion and candor will build mutual respect, strengthen relationships and increase a team's commitment to its leaders.

Clear, concise and personalized speech

The most effective way to speak is also the simplest! Speak in a clear voice, and don't rush your delivery. Keep your vocabulary simple and use your words economically. Make sure the person or persons to whom you are speaking have your full attention, holding eye contact to reinforce your attentiveness. Use their name(s) as you speak to them.

When they speak, acknowledge you hear them and listen! Ask questions to learn and gain an understanding of their message.

Robert was not a gifted communicator and the pressure of his sales management assignment was adding to his communication woes.

Several months of missed revenue plans had left him irritable and feeling overwhelmed. Communicating with his team was painful. He knew they had little regard for his professional status. He blamed them for failing to make plan—they blamed him for everything! He was beginning to doubt his ability to manage this sales team. Most of the sales staff had already lost what little confidence they had in him. Conventional wisdom had Robert as a soon-to-be casualty.

"Not as easy as you thought?"

"No. It has been difficult."

"That's because you're making too many beginner mistakes." Al Winters was a solid VP of Sales; but it had taken him several failures and 20+ years to reach a solid level of competency. At 69, his watch was about over, his real challenge was to find a successor...soon!

"I hired you because you said you would do whatever it took to become a sales manager. Remember?"

"I do remember."

"Still committed or do you want out?"

There was a long pause before Robert replied, "I'm not a quitter and I'm not going to quit now!"

"Good, because you are going to need that resolve to succeed. For starters, you and I are going to work very closely and we are going to have a weekly list of tasks you must accomplish."

"Okay."

"This week, I want you to sit down with every member of your team, in private, out of the office. Ask them what you can do to help them succeed. You will admit you've gotten off to a slow start. Acknowledge that you appreciate their patience and really want their personal advice on getting things back on track! Then you will listen..."

"But I'll lose face with them."

"Robert, you need to get past the 'I'm the boss' stuff. Focus on

25

being a leader, which means you must have followers. They all know what your title is and they don't much care! What they expect is leadership and until they see that...you are not important to their real challenges."

Al slid a brochure across to Robert. "Leaders communicate with their teams, day-in and day-out on big and small issues. They build relationships and trust! Your second assignment is to attend this public speaking course. You need to work at more than public speaking, but it will help improve your ability to communicate with everybody."

"Am I being placed on a get-well plan?"

"Informally, yes! If I see some significant improvement, we will just consider this normal coaching. Robert, you and I are going to be working very closely. I am going to be in contact with your salespeople and will be asking several of them to help make this work...for everybody's benefit. Final topic for today...tell me what you know about the four constituencies every sales manager has..."

Robert offered a blank stare.

Engage each audience!

We have discussed the importance of communicating with your sales team. There are other audiences sales managers interact with—prospects and customers and their colleagues at the business. Colleagues may be in different departments, divisions, locations, and may work as peers, subordinates or superiors. The executive management team at your business is also an assembly to whom you must effectively communicate. Each of these groups can and will impact a sales manager's achievements and overall performance. Each constituency is important in its own right and deserves to be a focal point of your communications.

Al Winters called Karen to his office. "Got a nice e-mail from a customer expressing their appreciation for the time and information you have shared with them."

Karen nodded warily.

"I also had a nasty visit from Sydney Day. She believes you set her up as the fall person in your presentation to the executive committee last week."

"Well, I'm sure she will be back before too long!"

"Why?"

"I just had another run-in with her. Engineering is delaying the release of the SC6000 until next year. I have no way to make up the revenue short-fall this presents. Sydney wants me just to pretend the product was never released to the sales team. Al, I'm not trying to get her. I am just not going to re-write history to cover her problems!"

"Have you told the customers yet?"

"No. I am going to need your help with that. They are going to take this very badly. Two of the accounts are already grumbling about damages and legal repercussions."

"Why don't you let me kick this problem upstairs?"

"Fine."

"Call Sydney and tell her I am going to talk with the owners about the problem. Give her a heads up, be apologetic and sympathetic. Ask her if she has any alternative solution, stop making her the bad guy."

"Why are we all stepping around Sydney? This really is her mess."

Al stood up looked out the window and said in a quiet voice, "Sydney has bailed me out of more sales mistakes than I care to count. This is her mess, but she's part of our team and I'll do whatever I can to help her, which is what you should do also!"

"Oh!"

"Someday, you're going to need her help, so be very careful how you deal with this issue. Payback can be hell."

Karen left the office stinging from her first reprimand. This evening she would think about how to fix her Sydney problem. The immediate issue was deciding how to break this news to the customers.

Karen picked up the phone and dialed. It rang much too long before a sleepy voice answered. "Sydney, I'm sorry to call so late; but, I wanted to apologize for being...difficult. Could I meet you for breakfast tomorrow?" A convenient coffee shop was quickly selected.

Arriving right on time, Karen was surprised to find Al and the CEO of Baker Industries already deep in conversation with Sydney, who motioned her to their booth. "I invited Karen to join us. Whatever we decide, she has to explain to the customers."

Four audiences—each important communication targets.

How can I improve my skills?
Personal growth starts by acknowledging communication skills are important and then acting to improve those skills. Reading, educational opportunities and professional coaching will start you on your way. The interesting truth about the discovery and refinement of effective communication tools are the immediate benefits your progress will pay. Every little step you make is useful immediately!

The best communicators work at getting better! Most people are not born as great communicators, they achieve it from hard work and dedication. It may come easier to some than to others, but each of us has the ability to improve and keep improving.

In *Smart Selling! Your Roadmap to Becoming a Top Performer*, I remind readers that all sales communications should:
- Achieve the goal you set for the event.
- Result in learning by both parties.
- Help build a relationship.
- Reach agreement on the next step.

The advice is just as valid for sales managers as salespeople.

TEST YOUR KNOWLEDGE

1. When you learn to listen, asking questions comes easily.   True/False

2. Asking questions means you also have to answer questions.

   True/False

3. The value of consistency in your communications is important.

   True/False

4. Keep repeating the message...until _____!

5. The most powerful messages are communicated with:
   - ❑ Double speak and evasiveness.
   - ❑ Minimal details or specificity.
   - ❑ Passion and candor.
   - ❑ The knowledge that they must be repeated.

6. Sales managers have to communicate with:
   - ❑ Prospects and customers
   - ❑ Colleagues
   - ❑ Executive management
   - ❑ All of the above

7. Speak in a clear voice and don't rush your delivery.   True/False

8. The greater your vocabulary, the more persuasive you become.

   True/False

9. Make sure those to whom you speak have your full attention.

   True/False

10. The best communicators work at getting better! They acknowledge
    communication skills are important, then act to improve those skills.

   True/False

CHAPTER 2

Goals Are Paramount

If you do not have goals, you do not have a plan!
Sales managers without plans are certain to fail
sooner rather than later...

Effective sales managers understand the necessity of setting goals. They also understand that the real challenge they face is developing a portfolio of goals—strategic goals and tactical goals which encompass the responsibilities entrusted to their sales team and its support staff.

What is a goal? The dictionary tells us 'a goal is a thing for which an effort is made; something desired; an objective or target to be achieved.' Strategic goals are big picture endeavors—achieve an annual revenue plan or become the market-share leader for an important product or service offering. They are supported by plans, the ways and means by which you will make a strategic goal happen. Staffing plans, territory assignments, compensation plans all represent the tactical plans that are necessary for the achievement of the broader and strategic revenue goal.

I have always argued goals by themselves are of minimal value. Interesting but not conclusive. To be valuable and drive real achievement, your **Goals** have to be integrated with a plan to engage in those **Actions** which will produce the specific and desirable **Results** you can measure.

Goals—Actions—Results, a skill high-performance sales managers have learned to master and to communicate. Setting sales goals starts by determining the strategic business objectives you want your sales team to achieve. The goals are usually drafted in concert with the management team and should be aligned with the enterprise's overall business objectives. The sales revenue goal is typically the foremost strategic goal for which sales managers are held accountable. Other strategic goals can include customer acquisition or retention, customer satisfaction and the introduction of new business lines or products.

How do sales managers create strategic revenue plans?
Very carefully! Miscalculating your ability to reach a revenue goal will have serious implications for your business, your sales team and you personally. The pressure to commit to aggressive goals can be and often is very stressful. You want your sales team to achieve to its maximum potential, without being pushed past its ability to deliver fully to expectations. Remember, everything in the business planning process flows from top line revenue projections. Operating expenses, staffing, inventories and profits are all derived from sales projections.

The correct way to start is by examining your current plan and measuring how well you have performed to that plan. Are you at plan? behind plan? or perhaps, ahead of projections? Look carefully at the historical revenue trends the business has experienced and begin to adjust for the impact of...what has changed already or will be changed next year?

Will you have new products to sell? Is the sales team being expanded? Are you projecting your salespeople to be more productive and carry larger quotas? Is the business entering a new market? What is happening in your marketplace...growth, retrenchment or stagnation? How are the competitors faring? Is the pricing strategy for your products being changed? Literally, hundreds of questions to be asked, information to be analyzed and pro forma sales projections to be created!

The more senior your sales management assignment, the more responsibility you will be asked to undertake in creating the sales revenue goal. The VP of Sales in most businesses has an enormous amount of input and accountability for this strategic goal. The complete management team and the top executives will all participate. The discussions can often be difficult clashes between the proponents of growth and those favoring more deliberate risk taking, resulting in commitments and compromises across an organization.

What about tactical plans?
Tactical plans are the ways and means to support strategic goals. If you plan to substantially grow sales revenue, you may need to hire sales representatives and retain your key current contributors. Create a sales

staffing plan! The new hires will need to be trained, and existing salespeople may also require new skills to continue to achieve...a sales training plan! The channels you use to sell your products may be expanded or you may go international for growth...a sales channel plan! Tactical plans must include the actions you will take to create the measurable results you want.

Do not dismiss tactical plans as unimportant. Without the ways and means to support your strategic goals, your best laid plans will become little more than interesting statements. Creating, acting on and measuring tactical plans are the only way to make the 'big picture' goal work!

The alternative to having goals is?
The mistake busy managers often make is to ignore the need to establish goals. The error can be intentional or the result of inexperience. There may be some small amount of comfort from not being held accountable for any goals—my experience is that any relief is very short-lived.

Top sales managers understand an organization without a goal is a business which is reactive to countless distractions. Someone once described it as equivalent to trying to anchor a boat without having an anchor—works for a short while but not very long!

Without goals you have no way to know what actions to take or results to expect. You are then accountable for everything and nothing all at the same time!

Communicate the goals.
Having a powerful set of strategic goals and a portfolio of tactical plans will not achieve the results you want if no one is aware they exist.

Keep repeating your goals and measuring how well you are doing in meeting the prescribed results. The focus will bind and ground your team with a powerful set of common denominators.

Robert and Karen were both invited to attend the kick-off planning meeting for the new fiscal year at Baker Industries. Al Winters had stressed to each that the best use of their time would come from taking notes, listening carefully and learning! The meeting would last for three long days.

The CEO presented his vision for the goals the business was to achieve in the new fiscal year. He turned his attention to Al Winters. "Our sales revenue must grow at least 10% to generate the cash flow and profits we will need to invest in new manufacturing facilities. Al, your team will have to stretch next year and figure out how to reach this goal. You will have to get creative!"

Al responded to the challenge with a mix of emotions, "We will work on a plan to get you 10% growth...but, I want you to understand you are asking for a very large increase in sales. In the last five years, we have averaged 4% growth, with 7% our best performance."

The group broke into smaller taskforces to work on each of the strategic goals. The majority of Baker's senior managers attended the sales revenue deliberation.

The CFO lead a discussion of sales results for the current fiscal year, "Our sales are 3% behind plan YTD and the forecast is not encouraging for this quarter. I have to be candid, the results have to pick up quickly for us to even approach our historical 4% jump next year."

The VP of Marketing presented next. "The economists are predicting flat market growth for the next 24 months. Later this decade, demand should rise about 6% per annum. The industry has excess capacity currently. Our consultant's newest study shows none of our top three competitors are expected to grow more than 2% this year. In fact, if we make the current plan, we'll have the strongest growth rate of the Big Four."

The CFO chimed in, "Let's not forget the consultants have been optimistic in every annual forecast we have received in the last five years."

The CEO had heard enough, "Look, we have the opportunity to grab true dominance in our industry with one big push! I want to hear about how we can exceed our past performance...not why we can't do any more than we are doing! I was at a meeting last week to review the SC6000 issue. Just fixing that one problem could have changed our financial picture dramatically. Start thinking out of the box!" He got up and left the room.

Al Winters followed him out. "I want to remind you of our discussion last month."

The CEO glanced inquisitively at Al, "What?"

"I am going to retire by mid-year."

"Al, I can't talk you out of this?"

"No, it's beyond my control."

"So what's next?"

"We need to hire my replacement...and we need to reduce your expectations so the new VP of Sales has a fair opportunity to get established."

"10% won't work?"

"No, sir, it will not work, with or without my retirement!"

"I need to think about plan B—the acquisition strategy we discussed earlier this month."

"Yes, sir. In the meantime, I will reset the goal at 2% to 4% growth."

"Thanks, Al. I like 4%...but just get it right, okay? Tell the CFO I need to see him."

Al returned to the table and began to manage the goal setting exercise.

"Robert and Karen, you both need to have a first-draft revenue plan for next year by 7 p.m.—project best and worst case numbers. Let's go through the 'what changes' assumptions you are to use..."

Both Robert and Karen projected a 10% sales growth. Al began to drill down on their assumptions one point at a time. The discussion was lively, far reaching and at times argumentative.

"Robert, how are you going to sell 36 units of the SC6000 when the production line is targeted to deliver only 24 units?

"Expecting a new hire to be on board and at quota in 30 days may be a little aggressive!"

"Karen, you realize there is no marketing plan or budget for attending any conventions?"

The full management team initiated the new sales managers to the planning exercise.

"Karen, this projection has each sales representative at plan, and two new people at a partial-year plan?"

"Yes."

"How long have you been in sales?"

"Ten years."

"How many times in those ten years have you observed every sales person on a team making plan?"

"None!"

"Karen, the good news is, you have exposed the 10% growth plan as unrealistic...and you still have 12 hours to get the next draft to the point where you are willing to bet your job on delivering the projection!"

When Karen and Robert left the room, Al remarked, "They learned a lot today...let's see how they adjust tomorrow!"

The second day was not any easier. Robert tried to insist that he could reach 10% growth. Karen reset her goal to a 3% growth projection. The difference between the two sales managers was becoming apparent.

The VP Marketing summed it up, "Robert wants to please and he will go to extraordinary lengths to win approval. He can't explain how he will achieve his plan, but he wants us to know he believes he can do it...if we order it!"

"Karen, on the other hand, has some real financial and organizational acumen. She knows her plan will disappoint our CEO, but it is reality-based and defendable. She reset quickly after yesterday's grilling. I suspect she figured out we have ruled out the 10% target and moved to get her team a good plan. I bet she would accept a 4% or 5% growth target with little concern."

A lively debate followed before the group reached unanimous consensus—3% revenue growth for the next fiscal year would become the primary strategic sales goal at Baker Industries.

Al closed day two with the agenda for the final day. "Let's put together the tactical plans for sales staffing, sales training, territory assignments, sales representative compensation, and business development. Set each goal, your actions and measurable results."

His final advice was, "The time we have spent, and will spend, creating our strategic goals and tactical goals is effort well-spent. It will focus and guide all of our efforts next year!"

TEST YOUR KNOWLEDGE

1. If you do not have goals, you do not have a plan! True/False

2. What is the definition of a goal?

   ----

3. The sales revenue goal is the foremost strategic goal for which sales managers are held accountable. True/False

4. Tactical plans are:
   ❏ Big picture goals.
   ❏ The ways and means to support strategic goals.
   ❏ A distraction to most sales managers.
   ❏ None of the above.

5. Having a powerful set of strategic goals and tactical plans will not achieve the results you want if no one is aware they exist. True/False

6. The alternative to having goals is_____

7. Miscalculating your ability to reach a revenue goal has serious organizational repercussions. True/False

8. To drive real achievement, your_____have to be integrated with

   a plan to engage in those_____which will produce specific

   _____you can measure!

CHAPTER 3

Motivating A Team

I suspect you would have a difficult time finding a sales manager who did not want a motivated sales team. Paradoxically, many managers simply don't know how to get their teams to this state. We have already discussed the two important steps in motivating a team—communications and goal setting! The focus of this chapter will be 'why is a motivated team so important?' and also 'how do you create a motivated team and keep it motivated?'

Motivation! An incentive or inducement to action. Yes, the very same action that turns goals into measurable results. Remember your high school physics and Newton's Law of Inertia? Things at rest tend to remain at rest, things in motion tend to stay in motion. Motivation gets things moving and keeps them moving—including individual salespeople and sales teams.

Why is a motivated team so important?
A mentor remarked, *"Salespeople get paid to make things happen!"* I understood the concept at a personal level as a hyper-active salesperson, but when I became a sales manager, I really came to appreciate the wisdom of those words. Here is what I discovered.

Motivated teams will:
- Generate activity, enthusiasm and team work.
- Expose your prospects and customers to their excitement.
- Reinforce and feed off their own momentum.
- Raise the achievement bar for each and every member of their team.
- Make their sales managers job much easier!

Salespeople and teams lacking motivation will:
- Fracture into cliques with personal agendas.
- Focus on internal news and company gossip.
- Struggle with performance objectives and achievement.
- Frustrate and challenge their sales managers!

How you create a motivated team and keep it motivated!
The sole responsibility for motivating a salesforce falls squarely on sales management. You are the chief motivation officer! You create enthusiasm through direct appeals which clearly reinforce the behavior you expect. You, then, continually reward those who embrace this preferred behavior.

I inherited (on several occasions) sales teams which could at best be described as failing and lethargic. They were just plain unhappy and it showed! After countless hours of communication focused on positive reinforcement and goal setting, I turned my attention to the next objective—motivation.

You motivate unhappy salespeople one small positive step at a time. I emphasize the word 'positive' because it is so important for leaders to exhibit this quality. A sales team must buy into your efforts to create an environment that is conducive to success! The more people who believe in your efforts, the easier the task becomes. Success begets success and motivation begets more motivation.

The first motivation step is to take the focus of your team off the failed past or present and work on a brighter future...which starts now! You will need to fix or change the issues that are perceived as motivational drags—policies that don't work or rules which represent failed efforts. Why? Their continued presence serves little value and they will constantly be a negative drag.

Every failing sales organization is beset with challenges. I urge you to take a hard look at success inhibiting issues, and get the major roadblocks out of the way...quickly! Fixing these mistakes sends a clear message—the past really is behind. The message and your actions will speak volumes about leadership and motivation.

The second motivational step is to reward the achievement of positive results. Use your tactical goals as the basis for bonuses, incentives and recognition. Who made the most telephone calls to prospects this week? Who closed the most business today? Everybody who closes a sale this week gets a round of golf or tickets to a show. Offer an incentive for sponsoring new employees! Actions which are fun events, financially valuable and get every team member's attention—these drive motivation.

Your rewards program does not always have to be about money. Simply acknowledging someone's efforts in front of his/her peers can be a powerful incentive. Use your creativity to come up with countless ways of saying, *"Good job! Way to go!"*

The third step is to keep the momentum moving forward. Motivation is not a one-time event; it's a continuous stream of actions. Keep checking the team's motivational quotient and apply more or less activity as it rises and falls.

Ultimately, as the chief motivational officer, you set the pace by your communications, goal setting and presence. Engaging, challenging and monitoring your sales team is part of your daily responsibility. They need to see you and hear from you because you are the leader of their team. Roll up your sleeves, create the environment your team needs to achieve.

Al Winters called a sales meeting to announce the hiring of a new Senior Director of Sales, Norton Fields. He also announced his own transition into retirement within six months.

Norton had been recruited from a larger competitor, AG International. He had competed directly with Baker Industries for the last five years. As VP of North American Sales, he knew the industry and market inside-out. Al's retirement positioned Norton as his successor, but the choice did not come without reservations.

Dan Kelly, the CEO of Baker, peered anxiously at Al, waiting for an answer. "Do you like this guy?"

"Dan, he has a great resume, solid references and a MBA from a top school. I think he's really bright, should get up to speed quickly."

"He just seems arrogant...full of himself."

Al laughed, "I remember people saying the very same thing about you! Looks to me like they missed that call!"

"Okay...but keep him on a short leash for a while. Maybe I'm just being overly cautious. He's not someone I would..."

"Dan, just remember, he's a sales manager not a public relations manager, he may just be nervous—you can do that to people!"

Bob Kelly sat expressionless and left with Al. "Dan's not comfortable with the choice."

"Look, the candidates are all imperfect. It's not like we have a unlimited amount of options or time."

Bob knew Al was done with the discussion and the decision. The elevator stopped—Al exited swiftly. "Thanks Bob, lunch on Friday? Look, Norton may never win a personality contest, but he will do just fine."

Karen and Robert now had a new boss. They each reacted to the announcement quite differently.

Karen regretted the news of Al's imminent departure, because she had come to respect his leadership. She also knew Norton quite well...she had worked for him for several years. Karen resolved to keep her feelings about Norton to herself. The crowd at her door would be asking her to give them the gossip about the new heir apparent.

Robert had a smile from ear to ear. Al's soon-to-be departure would remove a 600-pound gorilla from his back...or so he thought. "Surely Norton will have other things to do than supervise me on a daily basis!"

It took Norton about a week of discussions with salespeople and the support staff to figure out Robert's sales team had a major motivation problem. He knew how to fix motivation issues...his plan started with Karen. "You know, you were the best sales rep we had on our team!"

"Yes, I was."

"You're on your way to becoming a good manager."

"Thanks."

"So, don't get insulted if I ignore you while I focus on fixing the real problem around here. Okay?"

"I'm fine with that, Norton."

"Karen, what's your opinion of Robert?"

"Oh, he's very decent and pretty inexperienced."

"Anything else?"

"No, Norton, there's nothing else. I'm sure you'll decide to do whatever is necessary."

"Karen, you still don't trust me. Do you?"

Karen got up and moved to the door, she paused just long enough to lock onto Norton's eyes. "No reason not to trust you, is there?"

"What?"

She closed the door and in a measured voice addressed Norton. "I watched you turn AG inside out."

"That's right, I shook the sales team by the collar and got rid of salespeople who didn't perform or couldn't get motivated."

"No, you got rid of people you didn't like, everything else was just a secondary consideration."

"I built an enthusiastic team to help me run the company, just like I intend to do here. You can be part of my team or not, that's your decision! But I don't have a problem with you!"

Karen forced a smile. "Careful, Norton, this is a different organization, you will learn not everybody will be so easy to manipulate."
She left the office, her blood pressure steadily climbing into the stratosphere.

Norton picked the phone up and dialed Dan Kelly. He left a voice message for his employer, "Hi Dan, Norton Fields, I noticed you and I both belong to the same golf club. One of the members told me you are just starting to play. In another life, I aspired to be a professional. It would be a pleasure to give you some help with your game and discuss a little business along the way. Here's my home number..."

"Your team is not exactly a bunch of happy campers are they?" Norton had Robert's full attention. "Sales teams that lack motivation almost always fail, and they take their managers and companies down with them! You can motivate them positively or with fear, which will it be Robert?"

"Positive motivation, of course."

"Good! What are the three biggest obstacles to success from their perspective?"

"Paperwork, a lack of prospects and product deficiencies."

"What's your plan to address their concerns?"

"Well, I'm not sure there's really all that much I can do, other than encourage them."

"Let's assume your encouragement is not working...what then?"

"Look, I'm not a babysitter. They have to take responsibility for their own success...right?"

"No...wrong! You have to lead them to achievement, not watch them flounder. Your job is to set goals, push them, encourage them and coach. In other words, motivate! Then, you measure their results and make adjustments in the game plan."

Robert was stunned. Within a week, he had established a taskforce to reduce any and all needless paperwork. He moved out of his office and took a desk on the sales floor. The walls were adorned with a large charts tracking each salesperson's daily sales and new prospect contacts.

A set of new golf clubs sat on a counter awaiting a new home.

"Okay, today we're going to find a good home for these Turf Master Clubs. Our winner this week made over 200 telephone calls and netted 26 new prospects—2 of which have already become new customers! Ned, come up here and introduce yourself to your new clubs and tell everyone how you pulled off this feat!"

Robert announced, "Next week's contest is about closing business! The team member with the most gross sales will be enjoying a weekend in Las Vegas."

Someone shouted, "It's mine...don't even think about winning this one!"

Norton watched the excitement and realized Robert had began to turn a corner. He observed, "Still a long way to go, but the first signs of motivation are beginning to appear!"

TEST YOUR KNOWLEDGE

1. Motivation gets things moving and keeps them moving!   True/False

2. Motivated teams will:
   - ❏ Generate activity, enthusiasm and teamwork.
   - ❏ Raise the achievement bar.
   - ❏ Expose prospects and customers to their excitement.
   - ❏ All of the above.

3. The sole responsibility for motivating a sales force falls on the individual salespeople.   True/False

4. You motivate unhappy salespeople one small positive step at a time.   True/False

5. Salespeople and teams lacking motivation will:
   - ❏ Work out their issues in time.
   - ❏ Exceed plan despite the challenges.
   - ❏ Fracture into cliques with personal agendas.
   - ❏ Focus on internal news and company gossip.

6. When you inherit or have a failing team, you must:
   - ❏ Take the focus off the failed past or present.
   - ❏ Terminate everyone not at plan.
   - ❏ Maintain the current status quo.

7. You motivate a team when you reward the achievement of positive results.   True/False

8. Motivation is not a one-time event!   True/False

9. Motivation is not always about money.   True/False

10. The Chief Motivational Officer is also known as the _____

CHAPTER 4

Coaching Performance And Achievement

Salespeople need to be directed...which sales managers accomplish through coaching.

What is a coach? —someone who teaches, tutors or mentors. The results managers expect from their coaching are improvements in performance and achievement. Coaching may be done one-on-one or it may be conducted in group settings. It involves teaching and learning life skills, business skills, ethical behavior, policies and procedures, product information and hundreds of other points of knowledge and behavior. Sometimes coaching can be easy and enjoyable; on other occasions it can be difficult and confrontational. The lessons coaches teach are presented and ultimately learned in many different forums, and no one has a monopoly on doing it correctly!

Coaching does not focus only on salespeople who are struggling, it reaches out to every person on a team...because we can all achieve more and perform at higher levels! The important thing for managers to remember is that the best coaching is planned and premeditated. It starts with this question: What do the team and individual salespeople need to improve upon in order to advance their ability to perform?

Occasionally, coaching will be done spontaneously and in real time. The moment presents the need to correct or refine a sales skill, review the thought behind a decision or react to an important event. A learning opportunity is front and center and can't be ignored!

Where should I start my coaching?
Start with fundamental skills and disciplines and then advance towards more refined concepts. Challenges—such as prospecting, qualifying, time management and working to a sales methodology—are often big payback skills. Teaching sales practitioners why or how CEOs and business owners are their primary audience and what message to deliver is far more valuable than teaching them assorted tricks to schedule meetings successfully. Why? People who have meetings for which they are unprepared don't often succeed!

When you communicate with and actively engage a sales team, you will learn first hand their skills and limitations. I always made calls with my salespeople. I observed their sales skills and interactions with prospects, which gave me a real sense of individual competency. Do this enough and you quickly discover who needs what kind of coaching, as well as what the larger team can do to improve its performance.

48

Here are some basic questions you can ask yourself to help get a coaching agenda started:

- How experienced are my salespeople?
- What is their performance history?
- Are they asking for specific types of assistance? Why?
- What have you observed and measured about their performance?
- What are your business partners, prospects, customers and other interested parties witnessing and reporting?

A sport's analogy...new coaches watch film of their teams, ask other coaches for observations, learn from practice sessions, speak with sports writers, former players and their current players. All this is compiled with an eye to building a coaching plan designed to improve the team and individual players. They watch, listen, learn...and then act!

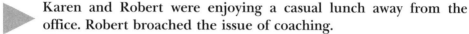

Karen and Robert were enjoying a casual lunch away from the office. Robert broached the issue of coaching.

"You seem to really be good at coaching. I keep hearing your salespeople saying things like: 'Go ask Karen'...'Karen said I should'!"

She delighted at the thought someone was actually taking her advice. "I keep a list for each salesperson of what they do really well and what needs improvement. We regularly discuss the list and how they are progressing. When I think they have shown significant improvement in a particular area, I congratulate them for the accomplishment."

"How did you create this list?"

"A lot of it comes from personal observations of their work, and I ask them what they think are the skills and issues holding them back from achieving their full potential."

"Do they get upset with criticism?"

"Sometimes. I try to keep my comments very positive so they stay motivated. The whole idea is to help them become better salespeople. I keep reminding them of that simple fact!"

"Some of my people don't seem to want to know what I think!"

"The thing I have found about coaching is they have to know you are truly committed to their success. If they question your commitment, then they will shut you out and try to coach themselves."

Robert paused as if in pain, "The thing is, some of these people have a lot more sales experience than I do."

"I understand. Why don't you start with something you are really good at and focus on coaching that skill?"

"Well, you know, I am super-organized and a great time manager. I could start there."

"Sounds to me like a great way to build some credibility and rapport with your team! Just keep in mind that every sales manager has strengths and weaknesses. Nobody has every answer!"

"Thanks, Karen."

"Anything else I can help with? It's important to everyone that your team achieves plan."

"You could well benefit if I fail."

"No, not really Robert."

"If you were making a list of the things I needed to improve, what would you tell me to work on?"

Karen had discovered a side of Robert she had not seen before. She offered him some advice but was very careful not to be judgmental or appear critical of his efforts. She knew he was struggling to find his way in this assignment.

Coaches must be beyond reproach.
The power to influence performance and achievement comes from:
- The position you hold.
- The professional experience you have accrued.
- The ability to provide leadership, create goals, motivate and embrace change.
- Your personal credibility!

Salespeople want to trust, respect and be coached by their sales managers, unless they are given cause to reject those efforts. Unfortunately, salespeople learn from personal experience and their peers. Not every sales manager provides value or can be trusted! They are often wary and skeptical about new managers.

Coaches must earn respect and then guard it jealously! I believe the quickest way to build credibility is to tell your sales team the simple truth—your job starts with making them successful. Everything begins and ends with their individual and collective performance and achievements. Then, live up to your promise day-in and day-out! Just holding a position or having experience by itself will not create the personal credibility successful coaches enjoy. Leadership skills are essential, as is the ability to set goals and motivate, but...

**Salespeople must believe in
your commitment to work selflessly for their success.**

Until you are prepared to put your personal agendas aside and focus your efforts on your team's growth and performance, you will not truly become or reach acceptance as a coach. A lot of very smart and successful salespeople never become sales managers because they are not willing to make this important transition. Not surprisingly, many sales managers fail because they also can't accept or function as a coach.

Sales teams will respect the natural desire to achieve recognition for your own efforts as long as your success comes from their success. They will not tolerate misguided coaches who attempt to succeed somehow at their expense or in spite of a team's failure!

Coaches need a healthy sense of humor and patience.
Why? Because laughter is a much better medicine than anger. As a coach, you want people to accept your advice and then act on it. Unfortunately, accepting and acting on well-given advice is not always something that happens.

I can vividly recall being in wood shop as a teenager and having a frustrated teacher explain for the umpteenth time how to use a wood plane. Try as I did, I could not grasp the correct way to use the tool. My teacher in exasperation exclaimed before the entire class, "Tom, no one can be this dumb!" I remember being thoroughly embarrassed but replying, "I know, but I guess I really am this dumb!" Laughing hysterically, he offered tutoring so we could both be embarrassed in privacy! I hate to admit this, but coach never did get me to be very proficient with a wood plane.

Your patience will be tested when you give advice again and again only to see it rejected, forgotten or remain beyond someone's ability to execute. Far too frequently, you will have to repeat this advice before it sinks in or a proverbial light comes on! Occasionally, the wisdom you are communicating is beyond the will or comfort zone of your audience and will never be affected.

Every once in a while, someone will just reject your coaching—plain and simple. I have been told, *"Thanks for the advice, but...no!"* You will hear the same response in your career as a sales manager! When people reject your coaching, you have to decide how aggressive to become with the advice. As a sales manager, you will learn to love salespeople who want to be coached, and deal with those who don't. Often the very people who most need assistance are the first to refuse any advice.

Here are two approaches I have successfully used with resisters: First, the failing sales practitioners get advice which includes the following caveat,

"If you refuse to take any advice and continue to fail, I will have little choice but to assume you were okay with failing and leaving this team." The response is typically, *"What do you mean?"* Reinforce for your listener that something has to change for their personal performance to improve. Refusing to accept help or make adjustments sends a very bad signal to you and their peers.

Second, ask the salespeople whom you believe can and should exceed their current performance levels— *"Is it your goal to be a mediocre salesperson? Because I believe you can perform better than you are currently. My advice is about helping you improve to the next level!"* You will get their attention. Don't expect every salesperson to accept and act on your advice...but don't ever stop trying!

 Smitty was waving to get Norton's attention. "Before you leave...I need some advice."

Norton was already in the parking lot and stopped.

"I offered the deal we discussed this morning to Performance Printing."

"Yeah?"

"They essentially rejected it."

"Why? Did you offer them exactly what we discussed?"

"Pretty close...with some minor changes."

"Minor changes, what's that supposed to mean?" Norton, clearly upset, dropped his briefcase, glanced at Smitty and rubbed his forehead. "Look if you refuse to follow my advice to the letter...then don't bother asking!"

Smitty was taken by surprise. "I'm not a rookie, I exercised my best judgment but..."

Norton picked up his case and walked towards his car and muttered loud enough for Smitty to hear. "Salespeople! Just Stupid!"

Smitty could only shake his head and think, "First, Robert and now this character...some coach."

TEST YOUR KNOWLEDGE

1. A coach is someone who teaches, tutors or mentors.   True/False

2. Coaches should focus on struggling salespeople.   True/False

3. The power to influence performance and achievement comes from:
   - ❏ The position you hold.
   - ❏ Your professional experience.
   - ❏ Your personal credibility.
   - ❏ All of the above.

4. Coaches must earn respect and then guard it jealously!   True/False

5. Explain why coaches need a healthy sense of humor and patience.

_____

_____

_____

6. How should you deal with those who reject your coaching?

_____

_____

_____

Control The Selling Environment

Non-existent Control — Absolute Control

What is the selling environment? Why should sales managers control it? The selling realm is defined as 'the conditions in which salespeople operate and sales activity is carried out.' This setting has two components—the external one focusing on the customers and the internal one leading to a creative, efficient administrative process. The domain is rooted in both the physical and intellectual. Control of this working order is fundamental to the sales management assignment and the achievement of success.

Somewhere between—"Nothing gets done without my approval" and "I'm not interested in how you sell" is effective control.

The Internal Environment

It is difficult if not impossible to manage a sales team without a well-organized internal support structure. The primary goal of this effort is to allow salespeople to focus their selling time on prospects and customers and create a base of information which sales management can use to measure productivity. The first principle of sales environment control is:

> **Every salesperson, regardless of their product, territory or motivation, has a limited amount of time to spend with prospects.**

It may be 40 hours a week or 60 hours; whatever it is, you want their focus on that selling time. Why? Because it's the only time they can fulfill their real mission...selling! Don't allow or encourage the internal sales environment to encroach on selling time.

The challenge comes when you attempt to manage under this principle. Unfortunately, it is very enticing to spend valuable selling time in meetings, creating forecasts, finishing expense reports and participating in legitimate information exchange activities. The more bureaucratic the internal environment, the more selling time is consumed. The more departments or administrators make demands on selling time, the more critical the challenge becomes. The 40 or 60 hours we discussed earlier quickly becomes 10 or 15 hours!

I want to be clear—good intentions and valid business purposes aside—this classic dilemma creates a lose-lose environment. The business, sales management and salespeople are all victims. Sales managers must decide what information they and other business functions really need, when they need it and how much selling time they are willing to sacrifice to obtain this data. Keep asking: What will this requirement cost us in lost opportunities and sales revenue?

The management of the internal sales environment requires:

Clear policies about business conduct, ethics and employment practices
Everyone on your team has the right and an obligation to learn and accept the principles your sales organization and business embrace. Salespeople deserve to know how you expect them to interact with customers, prospects, peers and the community at large. Behavior and ethics matter internally and with your external audiences. Leaving these crucial issues unaddressed or un-managed is extremely dangerous in today's litigious business climate. Be certain the policies and practices are in writing and available for everybody to examine.

Sales managers must be especially diligent to support these policies with their personal actions, directives and coaching each and every business day. What you say and do will have an enormous impact on the reinforcement of these policies.

Adequate business facilities and equipment
The facilities your salespeople work from and how they are equipped to sell and compete are important. The basics matter when it comes to a work environment. Clean, safe, well-lighted office space, with a little bit of privacy, impact both morale and performance in a positive way. Selling assignments are so diverse that you will have to tailor the facility to the type of requirements your business presents. Telemarketers will have a different set of office demands than sales reps selling high-end financial services.

Sales teams will require everything from office supplies, computers, specialized software, and internet access to credit cards, expense accounts and automobiles depending upon their assignment. Your budget and collective judgments about the efficiency and productivity of their selling time will help you determine how much capital to invest.

Limiting the ability of your sales team to perform by failing to invest in a suitable infrastructure is self-defeating. Budgets which constrain sales performance are short-term patches which seldom deliver desirable results.

The CEO of a company I worked for used to complain bitterly about the telephone expenses our very successful sales team incurred each month. He constantly questioned why we were always on the phone. The argument was ridiculous because his management team knew—less phone usage equated to fewer sales!

What he should have been asking was how our telecommunications network could have been re-configured to increase productivity and reduce costs. He just couldn't get past reducing the monthly bill by simply cutting budgets which were then ignored, because we needed to make our revenue plan!

Facility and equipment plans need to be crafted to maximize sales productivity while restraining unnecessary capital expenditures.

Channels to exchange information
Managers and sale representatives need forums to exchange information. The channels you select for conversations can range from face-to-face discussions, to using the phone, e-mail or text messaging. Scheduled meetings, conferences, off-sites and informal social gatherings are all valuable forums for discussions. Your team needs to know how they will receive information and how to get information to you!

Perhaps most importantly they need to know you value the chance to share information with them. The more communication you have with your sales team, the easier it becomes to anticipate and react to their needs. Leaders who are out of touch with the reality salespeople confront each business day soon lose the ability to exercise sound judgments.

Sales managers should work to encourage and achieve active dialogues with their salespeople. Leaders do not hide from learning good news or bad news and everything in-between!

In fact, they encourage communication and provide the necessary channels and forums...to make it happen!

Open doors to other internal business functions
Salespeople require access to peers and experts across an organization, just as other parts of your company will want to access information, opinions and support from the sales team. Sales managers are responsible for creating and maintaining these interfaces in a positive and productive manner.

Achieving a constructive balance requires work on everybody's part. Some organizational functions may choose to see the sales team as a source of additional work or advocating agendas they don't support. Sometimes the sales team wants to blame another department or function for making their assignment difficult. There is usually some truth and some fiction in each party's position. The bottom line—sales needs help doing its job and the organization needs both information and the market's feedback. Sales managers have to navigate the barriers to co-operation!

Grievance and dispute resolution

How do you resolve grievances? The answer is important because they will always exist in a sales organization. In my experience, a fair process for solving disputes is as important as the actual resolution.

Sales management is the first line in dispute resolution. Salespeople must have a clear escalation procedure beyond their immediate manager which allows them to present their dispute without fear of retaliation. The unvarnished truth is that many disputes will involve how you, as sales manager, applied the rules—which is why being well-organized and documenting the internal administration issues are so important. The fewer grey areas you have in policy or its application, the fewer disputes will arise.

Although the vast majority of salespeople want to be treated fairly and have the rules they are subject to applied equally, every team will have those who constantly push the envelope. They will present ingenious arguments to bolster their case to exempt themselves from or bend any and every rule. When you make exceptions to a policy, you should carefully consider the consequences. First, the exception will become common knowledge. Secondly, any and everybody who was subject to the policy you just revised will feel justified if not compelled to dispute the original decision they received. If you are going to change course, make it clear what the start date of the new approach will be; then, either grandfather the acceptance of or summarily dismiss the right to refile all past appeals.

Remember the old saying? *"The road to hell is paved with good intentions."* The wisdom applies to dispute resolution!

A sales administration and operations team

Managers need performance information and sales data to predict and respond to their business environment. Sales Administrators create reports that facilitate the monitoring of revenue projections—forecasts, pipelines, call reports and lost account information underlying a sales database— knowledge that needs to be collected on time and be organized effectively!

In addition to knowing how individual salespeople are performing, you need to know what they are doing. How many calls are they making each day, week and month? How many suspects become qualified prospects? How many prospects become customers? What's the number of customer interactions required to make a sale? How are the prospects responding to value propositions and proposals? What deals have the competition won? All this information help manage the metrics of the sales environment— the topic we will explore fully in our next chapter.

Salespeople also need a support function to handle a multitude of administrative or housekeeping issues: How do I get expense reports paid? How do I request time off? Who sends the package of brochures to this prospect? Where can I find our new marketing piece? These are the administrative tasks you zealously want to prevent from consuming selling time...but need to get accomplished! This function is easy to dismiss, but its value is both real and significant.

 The mood in Al Winters office was glum. Robert, Karen and Norton were all uncomfortable.

"Three salespeople have resigned...why?"

Norton took the lead in explaining the problem, "Robert's team is struggling. Karen's team is actually over plan. So it's really isolated in this one group."

"Why only Robert's team?"

"Al, I am going to be very candid. Robert is not ready for this responsibility. He's trying very hard, but you shouldn't have hired him. I have to say, you really left me a mess. I know our CEO's not going to be happy about this."

Robert flinched, Karen stared into her hands and Al was about to erupt. He leaned forward and glared at his senior sales director.

"Norton, you told me you had personally assumed the day-to-day management of Robert's team. It appears to have had little positive effect!"

"I have assumed daily management, believe me it would have been far worse without my involvement!"

Norton did little to hide his contempt for either Al or Robert.

Don Brown had worked for Al for over 8 years and made his sales plan without fail each year. They knew each other quite well...well enough to be brutally honest! Don made time for Al's invitation to lunch on short notice. Actually, he knew the call would come and that Al would have some questions about his resignation.

"Don, I can't believe you're leaving! Why?"

"I need some time off. Things are crazy right now, I can't make any money and I'm not actually enjoying myself. It's time to reset and then decide what's next."

"So, you don't have another job?"

"Al, I can get another job. The issue is I can't tolerate the sales management problems you have. Tell me I can transfer to Karen's team and I'll reconsider; not a promise, but I would consider it."

"Is Robert that difficult?"

"No, actually I like him, he's smart and has decent character. He's pretty green, but you knew that when you hired him...we all knew from day one. He is making slow progress as a manager from what I can see."

"So what's the problem?"

"Your designated successor is the problem."

"Norton?"

"Yes, sir. We call him the Chief Bureaucrat-in-charge. Al, this guy has meetings to review our accounts daily, meetings to review the forecast weekly, meetings on Monday to review the plan for the week, meetings on Friday to summarize the weekly progress, forms to request travel, sales call reports within 24 hours of travel and—my personal favorite—a mandatory telephone call after I leave a prospect's office! Last week, I spent a full two hours reviewing my expense reports with him. I've been in sales 10 years not 10 days! I have to tell you any selling progress we were making is now at a dead stop. There is no time to sell...absolutely none!"

"He isn't helping you?"

"Al, that's a very polite version. He is a control freak who is strangling the life out of this sales team! The resignations are just the tip of the iceberg!"

"He is trying to help, just so you know."

"I understand, but that is the worst part of this mess."

"I'll talk to Karen about a transfer, Don. We certainly do not want you to leave."

Al's next stop was Karen's office. He noticed the sales area was empty. "Where is everybody?"

"They're out selling. This is a key week, month-end you know."

"Any meetings this week?"

"No, why do you ask?"

"Seems to be a hot topic these days. Can you stop by my office after 5 p.m. today?"

Karen knew Al's moods well enough to realize this was not a good day or a social visit. He quickly told her about Don Brown and offered to transfer him to her team immediately.

"I would love to work with Don, but Norton is going to be very unhappy."

Al visibly stiffened and seem to bark, "Let me worry about Norton!

Make a deal with Don!" He regained his composure and then asked..."Tell me, how is your team organized internally?"

"The organization chart or how our internal administration works?"

"The administration."

"I have two basic policies. First, selling time is sacred and the administrative information I need is scheduled to minimize interruptions in selling time. Second, I have two sales administrators who manage the information process and schedule time for discussions with the sales team. I don't tolerate their requests being ignored by my salespeople! Most of the data collection is done via e-mail or the new sales administration system. Very little paper is created."

"What about meetings?"

"Pretty minimal, I use the phone for most account reviews when the account managers are traveling or between appointments and they e-mail me notes from the road...hotels, airports, on the weekends, etc. The sales administrators set up meetings when the salespeople are generally in the office, I work to their calendars. When I travel with them, there is plenty of time to review accounts, forecasts, performance statistics and just talk."

Karen got up and used Al's phone to call Gail Key, her senior sales administrator. "Could you bring the administrative package up to Al's office? We would like you to walk us through the basic material."

Karen reminded Al, "Gail is the most organized person I have ever met. She has complete responsibility for being sure the sales team gets what it needs from me and our company and I get the information I need as management. Please don't be too difficult..."

"Did you hire her?"

"Yes, I moved some travel and operating expenses around to fund the function and saved a few extra dollars on the new automobiles."

"Creative...you're doing quite a job. Are you enjoying it?"

"I really don't consider this work, but I know it is. Does that make sense to you?"

Before he could answer, Gail and her assistant arrived with laptops in hand. They methodically presented the information, which was collected annually, quarterly, weekly and daily from the sales team. The material included forecasts, sales call reports, lost account reports, pipelines, prospecting activity charts, contact information, expense information, individual calendars and sales performance measurements.

"I can sort and present the material in our databases any way that Karen needs it. Much of it comes in directly from the network our salespeople are all using. They can use laptops or a full menu of handheld devices to access the network and view the data for themselves. The idea is to use technology to allow the information to move back and forth without disrupting the selling time our people have."

"Meetings?"

"Well, Karen is a very hands-on communicator. So the meetings are really the ongoing dialogue she has with individual salespeople. We have one monthly sales meeting, generally the last Friday of each month, so everybody knows the restriction exists. They can be excused to close business; other than that, they all attend in person or by video conference. I do a formal agenda that Karen approves."

"What about Robert's team?"

"I don't support them, they have their own administrative system."

"Do you know anything about their approach?"

"It appears to be very informal from the conversations I have heard. Salespeople all do their own administrative stuff."

Don Brown and Karen were about finished with dinner as the waiter cleared the table, Don broached one final issue.

"Karen, I would love to work with you. I also have a long and close friendship with Bob Kelly and it would be fun to work with both of you. I'll stay for the rest of this year; but when Norton becomes VP of Sales, all promises are off the table."

Karen smiled and shook Don's hand, "So, we have a deal! Excellent!"

Al had Norton and Robert in his office by 7 a.m. A morning person, he enjoyed knowing his two friends were visibly struggling with the early hour. "I want you to install the administrative sales system Karen has adopted. Figure out how to hire whatever staff you need from your current budget, of course!"

Norton look dismayed but Al continued. "I've transferred Don Brown to Karen's sales team. I want the sales vacancies you have filled by the end of the month...unless you both want to go back into sales personally. Then, the three of us are going to meet at this time each morning to discuss how to smooth out the internal issues in your sales team and I want the salespeople back on the road and on the phone!"

The External Sales Environment

The next component of the sales environment is your interface with external customers and prospects. How do you sell to those who decide if your business prospers or falters? Far too many sales managers leave this most important part of the selling environment to chance or worse.

How salespeople go about selling is often ceded in large measure to each individual sales practitioner. The problem is they will each sell in a unique way. Some will succeed, others will fail and very little common ground will exist. Certain prospects will have good experiences, while others will be victimized by poor selling fundamentals and messages. The image of your business, its products and your sales team will be left to chance.

The alternative is to create a common sales methodology, a step-by-step roadmap of how each salesperson will manage their interaction with prospects and customers. I refer to this process as a **Business Sales Methodology.**

Why is it critically important? A business sales methodology will do a number of things for your team. It will:
- Lead all prospects, step-by-step, to the value they want and need,
- Monitor selling progress at an individual account level and for the entire portfolio of opportunities,
- Allow for analytic reviews of where, when and why you are encountering selling obstacles,
- Accelerate the closing of new business,
- Assist in managing finite selling time,
- Repeat the successes, limit the failures and present a unified message to prospects and customers!

As a sales manager, you limit the experimentation, cut your dependency on someone's intuitive sales practices, and build on proven selling skills executed in a pre-determined order with increased certitude. You will gain control of the most critical part of your assignment...creating sustainable and repetitive sales success! Everybody on the selling team works from the same playbook and knows how the plays are executed.

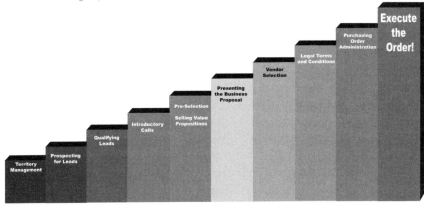

The Business Sales Methodology

Al Winters sat quietly in the meeting room. Perched on the window sill, he had a perfect view of the proceedings. Tough-skinned and well beyond embarrassment, he was nevertheless shocked. Karen's sales team was far superior to the groups he had personally supervised—in their organization, spirit and sales competence. How had she accomplished so much...so quickly?

As each person presented their accounts for the quarter, the approach they took was remarkable. "This deal is in pre-selection selling, I have created my selling message and my next step is to close for a formal presentation. I will need help when I present the business proposal later this month." Each member of the team understood where the sale being discussed was and clearly anticipated the next step. They frequently asked about the goals-actions-results being pursued.

A lengthy discussion led by product management and product marketing focused on fixing the message for the SC6000. "We are being eliminated too frequently in the introductory call stage. Our benefits need to have more specifics and better reference selling!" Very little arguing took place; instead, a real focus on correcting an acknowledged stumbling block was taking place. The management team from most of Baker Industries was in the room.

Karen and other senior salespeople offered their advice and exchanged information about sales approaches that were successful and others to avoid. The phrase, "Don't waste your time" was repeated again and again.

Bob Kelly and Don Brown erupted in laughter when a new sales rep mentioned a name they both knew well. "I understand he's the Comptroller, but trust me, Don and I spent hours trying to get a decision from him. Great guy, but he's not the executive buyer! Keep looking for the real decision maker...and don't buy into his promises. He means well, but he just can't deliver."

"Karen, where did this Business Sales Methodology come from?"

"Actually, Don Brown and Bob have been using this for several years. We adopted the concept from a book they both read, *Smart Selling! Your Roadmap to Becoming a Top Performer*. It's taught at a number of business schools. It has really allowed us to organize our approach to working with prospects. We have a common approach to selling, everybody knows what is expected of them, and it's great for the new people."

"They get trained quicker?"

"Yes, because the trial and error of learning what works and what to do next is really reduced."

"Any complaints about being too restrictive?"

"No, not really. We modified the methodology to fit our strategy. The concept was perfect because it really allowed us to use all common terms, have the same roadmap and it really helps with forecasting and managing the metrics."

"Managing the metrics?"

The 10 Steps of the

GOAL

1. Territory Management	Identify your potential accounts
2. Prospecting for Leads	Open a dialogue with target accounts
3. Qualifying Leads	Discover needs
4. Introductory Calls	Qualify and build momentum
5. Pre-Selection Selling	Sell your value—fulfill needs
6. Presenting the Business Proposal	Commitment from Executive Buyer
7. Vendor Selection	Verify the final steps
8. Legal Terms and Conditions	Finalize contract
9. Purchasing Order Administration	Get paperwork finished
10. Execute the Order!	Final order execution

Business Sales Methodology

ACTION	RESULT
Search all data sources	Territory knowledge
Hit the phones and e-mails!	Gain "Suspects"
Listen-Ask Questions-Learn-Analyze	Agreement your product meets a need!
FOCUS-ON-THEM!	Mutual agreement for evaluation cycle
Engage the Selling Pyramid	Present a business proposal
Meet the Executive Buyer	Selection of your proposal
Keep selling. Urgency matters!	Engage legal and purchasing for approvals
Get to the front of the line	Just internal paperwork remains
Leverage	Final internal approval
Set the date and time	Congratulations!

TEST YOUR KNOWLEDGE

1. The selling environment encompasses the conditions in which salespeople operate and sales activity is carried out.   True/False

2. The internal selling environment's primary goal is to:
   ❏ Keep everything documented and organized.
   ❏ Create administrative reports.
   ❏ Protect selling time.
   ❏ Reinforce management's directives.

3. Managing the internal environment requires:
   ❏ Clear policies for business conduct and ethics.
   ❏ Grievance and dispute resolution policies.
   ❏ Channels to exchange information.
   ❏ All of the above.

4. Sales must have broad internal support to do its job and the organization needs both information and feedback from the sales team. Sales managers are responsible for creating this spirit of co-operation.
   True/False

5. The external environment focuses on how you sell to prospects.
   True/False

6. What is a Business Sales Methodology?

_____

7. Why is a Business Sales Methodology important?

_____

8. Sales managers want to limit experimentation, cut dependency on someone's intuitive sales practices, and build on proven selling skills executed in a pre-determined order with increased certitude.
   True/False

9. Limiting the ability of your sales team to perform by failing to invest in a suitable infrastructure is self-defeating!   True/False

10. A sales administrative team will allow sales management to monitor how the sales team is performing and what they are doing. True/False

CHAPTER 6

Manage The Metrics

If you can measure it, then you can improve it.
Control of the selling environment, internally and externally, gives you the opportunity to begin to measure activities and correlate their occurrence with performance. You will discover certain sales activities lead to desirable results and others portend unsatisfactory outcomes.

The more you can demand, encourage and coach your team to embrace the activities that create success, the better your individual sales representatives and the collective sales performance. For example, if you discover and validate that successful salespeople make at least 50 new sales call each month, you have a target to insist each of your practitioners achieve. Why? It benefits them and it benefits your business.

How do I get started?
First you must decide what information is important for your business to measure. Each business, industry and market may have different needs and key indicators. I always recommend starting with modest requirements but focusing on criteria which you initially surmise can yield value quickly. The three broad categories of sales data:
- Activity-Related Measurements
- Transformational Measurements
- Prospect Feedback Measurements

Activity-Related Measurements
These measures tell you how many times someone performed a particular activity. Telephone calls, e-mails, sales calls, mailings, proposals, and presentations are all examples. The data may be collected daily, weekly or monthly. Who exceeds and underperforms the trend lines? What is the impact on sales performance? You want to discover, analyze and recreate the levels of activity which drive top performance. Activity-related measurements are a very common place to start gathering your sales metrics.

Suppose you find delivering high numbers of proposals distinguishes your best sales performers from the mediocre? You will want to act to increase the number of proposals individual sales representatives present! Perhaps high levels of mailings equate to success.

The experience you gain initially will help you to refine, re-examine and expand the base of information you need. The more you learn about the fundamental underpinnings to performance, the easier it is to lead your team to success.

Transformational Measurements

These are the movement of prospects from one step in the Business Sales Methodology to the next step. Salespeople are valued on their ability to deliver measurable results. The way they accomplish this task is to convert suspects to prospects and then persuade them to become customers!

How many cold contacts does it require to deliver a qualified prospect? How many prospects receive business proposals? What percent of those receiving business proposals become actual customers? Are the conversion rates the same for underachievers and top performers? Does time in a sales assignment impact conversion rates? Are the rates impacted by product, geography or time of year? These are just a few of the questions you'll need to answer in order to fast-track your team's path to closing business.

Prospect Feedback Measurements

What your prospects react to and disclose is important. Lost Account reports are an indicator of not only when, but also how frequently, salespeople are eliminated from competition. They can answer why you were dismissed. How many losses does your business sustain each week, month or quarter? Suppose you could prevail in 50% of those defeats by just changing something? The impact on your sales results could be enormous!

Call reports can offer the same type of insight. Is a new promotion program being perceived as valuable? What objections are being raised? Are top performers experiencing the same objections as the mediocre?

The range of measurements changes as you move from Activity to Transformational to Feedback. Activity-related measurements are very cut-and-dried, pure statistics. Feedback measurements are more subjective and require greater interpretative skills. Gathering the data for each form of measurement has its own distinct challenges.

Initially, mastering modest requirements will lead you to more complex and perhaps increasingly valuable information. Regardless of how sophisticated you become, all the material you discover will be individually and collectively valuable to managing and leading a sales team.

Controlling the selling environment creates the ability to mine the information necessary to manage sales metrics. Once you begin to explore and discover the underpinnings of your team's performance, you will learn that effective sales leadership is enabled by understanding reality and then executing change intelligently.

"Think of sales metrics as information or statistics that reveal what we do, how often we perform a specific activity, and if the activity is valuable to our salespeople and team," Karen explained to Al.

"Interesting."

"We're just starting to scratch the surface, but we have already discovered a number of performance indicators. Did you know the top quartile of sales performers all have several things in common?"

Before Al could answer, Karen rattled off her findings. "They make 25 cold calls each day on average. Their face-to-face prospect calls average 10 per week and they deliver 5 business proposals each week!"

"Top quartile...what about the bottom?"

"Don't ask, the activity levels are terrible. Less than 5 cold calls, 3 face to face. The good news is, I can now force them to face the facts and pick up the pace."

"I have also discovered that some of our people are very weak in moving prospects into pre-selection selling. They do great in the early stages of the methodology, but can't take prospects to the next step."

"I'm not sure I understand?"

"Okay, you know Stan Black? When you look at his cold calling and qualifying, he's off the charts. He gets on the phone and just keeps dialing, day-in day-out! But, his ability to convert his qualified prospects into those to whom he presents business proposals is terrible. In fact, only 10% of Stan's qualified prospects get to the proposal stage. Bob Kelly has a conversion rate of over 40%."

"Why?"

"I asked the same question. Stan finally admitted he is uncomfortable doing face-to-face calls which is a real problem, and he avoids doing the things you need to do at the prospect's office. His experience is basically telesales."

"Not one of my best hires."

"Well, Al, he may in fact be a great hire! I am going to team him with a salesperson who has exactly the opposite problem. Julie is great at closing the prospects she has; unfortunately, finding and qualifying is something of a challenge for her. If the partnering arrangement works everybody will benefit!"

"The metrics on Jason Smart were also very interesting. He is experiencing more competitive losses than any other sales representative by a factor of three. Business proposals are just being rejected! It really confirmed for me the impact of the relationship and business etiquette issues I have observed. He has some serious work to do if he is going to succeed."

"I was hoping some of his 'bull in a china shop' behavior would have disappeared by this time. Do you think we should try another round of counselling?"

"I need to take a few days to think about his future in sales."

"Karen, this is really good stuff!"

"It is! But remember, we're just scratching the surface!"

Al's mood grew solemn as he spoke softly, eyes fixed on his shoes. "Karen, I'm very impressed with your work, but I am personally disappointed you never warned me about Norton. Perhaps it's unfair but I am disappointed."

"Al, you never asked for my input—you just decided. I was placed in a no-win position. Would you have wanted me to complain after the fact? It was too late, wasn't it? I made the best of the situation."

"Okay...no hard feelings, Karen, I just wanted to clear the air."

"I have enjoyed working with you, Al, and I really don't want this to become a problem for us. You have your hands full, I understand that completely."

"I will promise you one thing—if I made a mistake, it will get fixed!"

TEST YOUR KNOWLEDGE

1. If you can _____ it, then you can improve it.

2. The three categories of sales data are:
   ❏ Prospect feedback measurements.
   ❏ Activity-related measurements.
   ❏ Transformational measurements
   ❏ All of the above.

3. List three examples of activity-related measurements:

   a. _____

   b. _____

   c. _____

4. Which are prospect feedback measurements?
   ❏ Call reports
   ❏ Pipelines
   ❏ Forecasts
   ❏ Lost account reports

5. What are transformational measurements? Why are they valuable?

   a. _____

   b. _____

6. Control of the selling environment creates the ability to mine the information necessary to manage sales metrics.   True/False

7. The best way to start to manage metrics is:
   ❏ List every activity the sales team is responsible for performing.
   ❏ Start with a simple set of activity-related measurements.
   ❏ Create statistics and prove them correct.
   ❏ None of the above.

CHAPTER 7

Hold Them Accountable For Results...

Every Day!

Top sales performers are often distinguished by the drive and intensity they bring to their job. They work at being successful every day, week after week! Their energy and commitment to being the best can inspire and lead a team. The results they deliver exceed plan each year. They understand and welcome accountability for results.

The reality sales managers face is simple—the majority of salespeople are not top performers. Some are solid professionals, others are mediocre producers and some are underachievers. They need to be coached, managed and pushed each business day to deliver results.

Sales managers are responsible for setting the pace for a sales team. Here is what I have learned—sales requires urgency, persistence and fearlessness. It is difficult and challenging work that offers substantial rewards for those who excel. Sometimes, salespeople decide to take the pressure of the daily hard work off themselves. They relax after a busy period for a few days or weeks. The grind of going through month ends, quarter ends, year ends, holiday buying seasons, hot summers and cold winters are all great opportunities to back off. Does a few days or weeks of down time sound unreasonable?

Be very careful how you answer this question! In fact, I will answer it for you...selling time is limited! Once you lose it, you can't get it back! This means a sales team and its individual members have to play hard every selling day. Sales management is responsible for making certain every salesperson uses every hour of selling time to the best of his/her ability!

▶ Al Winters sincerely liked Robert. He hired him and believed that in time Robert would become an excellent manager. Right now, however, he was about to deliver some stern coaching.

"Let's take a walk." Al, with Robert in tow, went down to Karen's sales floor. "Notice anything?"

"Quiet...nobody's here."

Al walked briskly to the administrative area and found Gail Key. "Karen around?"

"No, sir. She's in Los Angeles with David Wells and should be back in the office on Monday. I can page her."

"No, that's fine. David is our LA rep?"

"Yes, they are spending two days making sales calls together."

Al walked to the stairwell and turned to Robert, "Let's go tour your sales floor and see what's going on." He sprinted up a flight of stairs. The room was crowded and quite animated. A lot of heads disappeared into cubicles when the word of an Al sighting circulated. They stopped at the first workstation. Al sat down and began to ask his favorite question. "Sold anything today?"

Before his first victim could utter a response, he asked a second question, "Anything this quarter?"

"No, not yet, Al!"

"Why?"

"Well, I'm just getting started, setting up appointments, making telephone calls, getting organized after last quarter."

"Really, but last quarter ended three weeks ago."

"Right...you're right. I get the message."

Al stopped at each desk and asked the same questions before heading back to the staircase. His face flushed red, he turned to Robert. "What have you learned from our little stroll around the building?"

Before Robert could respond, Al with hands on his hips muttered, "Three weeks is 25% of a quarter! Three weeks spent celebrating a quarter they barely made! Three weeks into this quarter and in the hole."

"Sorry...my mistake."

"Robert, get them back to work...fast!"

"I will!"

"You have to learn to keep them focused each day on their assignment...selling! Don't let them go to sleep on you, because it will become an accepted way of doing business. We need every salesperson you have concentrating on their mission. Heck, it's hard enough without giving away time."

"Al, I feel like I'm harassing them."

"No, you're managing them. Until they get a clear picture of what you expect from them and respond positively to your message, your job is to keep reminding them! They may not like what you want, but their sales results will improve and they will all personally benefit!"

Al placed his hand on Robert's shoulder, "Look, they know you are new at this. Some of them are going to test you. That's why they were so nervous about my being here and asking questions. They know they're cutting corners! They're hoping to catch up later in the quarter. The problem is time will run out on some of them and then we all lose."

Robert's head was spinning...another day...another lesson.

Karen was having her own issues on the West Coast. Two days with David Wells can exhaust even the most energetic. Her eyes kept dozing as David negotiated Sepulveda Boulevard on his special back route to LAX. He was still talking and driving, answering the phone and honking at cabbies. "We made eleven calls in two days, not a personal record, but a good end to the week!"

"David, I'm not sure that includes the breakfast meeting and a few very interesting dinners. You should have a great couple of months!"

"I'm going to drop you at the terminal, park the car and we have one last conference call to make. We can do that from the club lounge."

"Who are we calling at 8 p.m. on a Friday?"

"Your friend, Mr. Ohono, we promised him some answers to his questions. I got them from Engineering and he agreed to give up some time this evening. I also booked you on the later flight...in case we ran late on the call."

Karen understood why David was a top performer...no quitting...just results! "Okay, let's go through your goal for the call."

The call did run late and Karen missed the last flight. "Well, now I need to find a hotel."

"No way, everything is long booked. My wife and I, fortunately, have a guest room for just these emergencies, and we provide free meals and airport transportation for all my sales managers. We will get you out of here first thing tomorrow morning."

"What, no Saturday calls?"

David laughed and shook his head, "Even I can't figure out how to get them to work weekends. Prospects...sometimes they just don't cooperate. But, if you want to review a couple of interesting accounts, nothing this quarter, but still opportunities..." He waited for a response, glanced at Karen and noticed she was already asleep.

Saturday morning came and went. David walked to his car after seeing Karen off. One more call to make and then he was done until Sunday evening.

"Kelly? The boss is on her way East. She sure made me money this week! I have to tell you the prospects really respond to her...smart businesswoman...personable and really likable. Actually, she has learned the products quite well, your training I assume?"

"What about...?"

"I couldn't get her to say a word about Norton. Nothing! My friend at AG Industries says the rumors are rampant. She is being heavily recruited to go back there as VP of Sales. You better talk to Al and our CEO. If you want me to help, I will!"

"I may need you to speak up."

"That's fine, I worked for Norton and I am not going to do that again! Nor do I care who I have to tell. I have invested too much time and hard work to sit by and watch this mistake. This company can do better than settle for any more second-rate sales leadership."

TEST YOUR KNOWLEDGE

1. Sales managers are not responsible for setting the pace for a sales team.   True/False

2. The majority of salespeople are not top performers.   True/False

3. Sales managers are responsible for making certain salespeople use their selling time wisely.   True/False

4. Sometimes salespeople decide to take the pressure of daily hard work off themselves and relax for the day, week or month.
                                                         True/False

5. Why is "Sold anything today?" an important question and reminder?

CHAPTER 8

Account Management

Account management focuses attention on the customers and prospects who are most important to a business. These accounts may be your best current customers or promising new prospects; the amount of product they purchase often represents a significant contribution to the revenue plan.

Sales Managers have a fundamental responsibility to lead account management planning sessions and progress reviews. I guarantee you will find yourself deeply involved with strategic and tactical account management activities! The plans have several important business objectives:
- Gather account information.
- Plan a strategy for each opportunity and key customer.
- Allocate business resources.
- Monitor the execution of the account plan.
- Consult on adjustments and course corrections.
- Win the business!

Sales representatives with responsibility for large complex accounts regularly create and follow formalized account management plans. In some sales organizations, every representative will be involved in account management exercises, while other sales teams may assign only a few senior salespeople to work their key account opportunities. The plans are often created annually and modified as needed.

Gather account information
Planning starts with the basic information you will need about each account. Who are they? How do I get in touch? Who is the contact for the account? Which key executives must we persuade? What products are under consideration? What quantities? What has transpired to date? This is the information on which you can build strategy and would be required to know if you had to reassign the account, or take personal charge tomorrow!

The material you compile should be created with an eye to minimally impacting selling time. Documentation takes time and it is an effort to keep current! Some salespeople are wary about revealing account details because it represents a disclosure of knowledge, which can be viewed as power. Their logic of keeping managers in the dark is simple—the less management knows the more flexibility I have and the more difficult it is to replace me!

The issue is commonplace and the answer is just as plain-vanilla; the information belongs to the business which is why managers require it and salespeople are obligated to provide it! Don't allow anyone to withhold or fail to disclose the information you need and want.

Plan a strategy for each opportunity and key customer

How will you win the business? Leadership, communication and teamwork is a good place to start! You may also want to read *Smart Selling! Your Roadmap to Becoming A Top Performer*, and *Winning Business from Difficult Competitors*, both authored by yours truly.

Accounts that are important to your business deserve a well-thought-out account management plan. The salespeople who manage these accounts should become experts about the organization they sell to and be able to lead an effective sales campaign. Planning also encourages teamwork and realistic appraisals of the strengths and weaknesses of each person, product, competitor and prospect. I encourage you to brainstorm with your account managers as you plot your way to victory account-by-account.

Much of the selling to major accounts will be team-driven. Drawing support from and beyond the sales organization requires planning. Each participant needs to have a specific and defined role. Why? The message you present to your prospect must be focused, coordinated and consistent. The power of a well-scripted sales campaign is enormous. Conversely, a sales effort that is disjointed and inconsistent is a sure loser! Sales managers and their salespeople are responsible for managing the teams that undertake complex and important crusades to win new business.

The initial account management plan you create is just a starting point. As you move through your sales methodology, the plan will be revised to reflect new developments, opportunities and challenges!

Allocate business resources

The value that comes from planning includes a proactive allocation of business resources. You develop a consensus of what people resources, events and special needs each prospect will require.

For example, the team may decide a particular account will be well-served by having a detailed presentation conducted by your engineering executives; another prospect may want to explore partnership arrangements with your marketing executives—resources to be allocated, briefed and coordinated! Suppose you have to host a series of visits to reference accounts...details and groundwork.

Allocations can also trigger financial decisions. A prospect requires a mandatory modification to a product before they will consider your final proposal. What will the modification dictate? Labor, material, engineering resources, production facilities, and delays in other projects—all of which have cost and pricing implications. You may decide to increase the cost of the proposal or pass on performing the modifications. Account management decisions are driven by the allocation of business resources.

Monitor the execution of the account plan

Very few account management plans go unchanged! Despite the best efforts of top professionals, prospects have a way of surprising and challenging even the best of blueprints. You don't want to micro-manage each account for your team, but you do want to be sure the plan is followed. Leaders encourage initiative and discourage careless or thoughtless decisions! The best way to be certain your account team lives up to its commitments is to verify the execution of their account management plans each step of the way.

I recall with great amusement a detailed plan I crafted to win an important new account. Armed with a support team, plan at the ready, I prepared for an introductory call with the CFO of a major financial institution. After our introductions, the senior executive hosting the meeting introduced his new Comptroller. The new executive asked but one question! "Tom, is this the same system I had at First National Bank?" My answer was a confident, "Yes, the exact same product!" He looked over at his boss, then said to me, "If you have a contract we can get this done right now and not waste your time or mine on another meeting."

My manager later commented, "Our plan didn't anticipate this twist, but you certainly responded well to the unexpected!" Not all surprises are as delightful!

Sales managers have on-going roles in the vast majority of account management plans.

One of my sales representatives, frustrated with his progress with a prospect, asked me to make a call to his account. We had worked long and hard executing the account plan step-by-step and cultivating relationships and eliminating competitors. In my view, our team had performed quite well!

An animated discussion ensued over whom I should telephone to find out what had delayed the final decision and how we could persuade that executive to execute the promised order. With my salesperson's grudging approval, I elected to call the President of the company, by-passing the General Manager who had recently become difficult to find.

I introduced myself and explained the nature of my call. Before I could finish more than a few sentences, the President asked, "Have you been promised a signed order?" My answer was "Yes, we were assured this step would be accomplished this week, but we seem to be having a problem getting a response." He then informed me, "The General Manager has signed a number of orders and promised other orders which were completely unauthorized and beyond the scope of his authority. I am sorry you were misled. We are neither in a financial position to honor the orders he signed nor to entertain any new proposals. The Board, in fact, terminated the GM this morning!"

Surprise...I can remember commenting that our plan had worked, with the exception of one detail—we should have introduced our offering to the prospect's president earlier in our campaign.

Sales managers have to establish a review process for each and every account management plan. Schedule your reviews weekly, monthly or quarterly and leave a little time for an emergency discussion along the way to closing.

Consult on adjustments and course corrections

Along with oversight must come a willingness to encourage adjustments and provide advice. Give your sales representatives credit for smart actions and refocus them when they miscalculate. The more you learn about the accounts, the better you can grasp the details, provide meaningful advice and support your team.

Sales managers can add a vital perspective to the challenge of managing important opportunities. Here's how: Sales representatives can become too close to and invested in their key accounts, they struggle to maintain their objectivity. Executing to plan slips in favor of cutting corners. The urge to get the deal done prevails.

Conversely, some salespeople bog down in detail, procrastinating on each step in the plan. Your job is to guide and focus their effort by providing a second opinion and encouraging them at each step in what can prove to be a long, complex and difficult assignment!

Win the business!

Planning account management strategy is imperative, but don't lose sight of one simple fact—every account management plan, each review, course correction and ounce of intellect, energy and teamwork you devote to the challenge of managing key accounts has but one objective, and that is: "Win the business!"

▶ Robert and Tad Smith were ready to discuss the final draft of Smitty's account management plan for Blue Stone Publishing. The account was one of Baker's largest customers and could be anticipated to purchase multiple presses once again this year. In fact, the rapid expansion of Blue Stone's Print-on-Demand client base in the Pacific Northwest was driving the need for a new plant in Washington state.

"Are they going to buy our new presses this year?" Robert inquired.

Smitty grinned. He noticed yellow highlighter and notes scribbled all over Robert's copy of the plan. "Robert, nothing is guaranteed, but it's hard to imagine they could avoid a purchase. They could relocate our older presses, but in the past when they built new plants, they chose new equipment."

"What model are you thinking about proposing?"

"Good, you cut to the key question! I'm leaning to SC6000s...I mean, how could I explain offering to sell them our older units?"

Robert had done his homework, "I was thinking, Smitty, maybe we should give them several alternatives. Get them debating which of our solutions they want and water down Triad or AG's impact."

"You mean we give Blue Stone the choice of 6000 or the current units?"

"Actually, I was thinking more about two new configurations, 6000s and 3600s—plus a third choice, reconditioned 3600s. Drop the price with each tier, allow upgrades for a couple of years."

"That's a great idea!"

Robert picked up his phone and called Sydney Day in Engineering. "Smitty and I could use your help on Blue Stone, and could you call marketing and round up the product managers for the 6000 and 3600 presses?" When he hung up, he volunteered, "Why don't you let me run interference for you internally, schedule the resources you need, coordinate references, set up meetings...so you can focus on the customer."

Smitty hesitated, this was a true leap of faith which he was being asked to make!

Robert continued on, "We should make a list of the people you want assigned to the account team, I can get them briefed on the strategy we are going to use to win the deal."

"Okay...let's have you run the coordination stuff. That means we are going to have to talk almost every day."

The comment wasn't lost on Robert.

Smitty continued, "Here's my take on the message we present and a first pass on the substance of our proposal..."

Karen did a double take. Then asked herself, what's Sydney doing here? She is supposed to be in LA with David Wells...she called Wells within minutes. "Hi, I thought Sydney was meeting with Mr. Ohono today?"

"I cancelled the meeting, Ohono dismissed the need to spend

more time examining the design of the SC6000."

"Really, but..."

"I know, it surprised me too. He decided he was good to go on the reliability issue and moved on to configuring the options."

"I still would have put Sydney in front of him."

"Karen, it felt like we were sending the wrong signal by continuing to explain our specifications. My instinct is he is really past the issue, I don't want to appear to be explaining and re-explaining something we believe he should be afraid of...especially since he's ready to move on."

"Okay, David. So what's next?"

"I have a conference call set up with product management to go through the XMS carriage option."

Karen waited and then he explained.

"I called Sydney last night, I was going to call you next, but I had a little accident on the way home."

"What happened?"

"Let's just say I wasn't paying attention and hit a taxi, rear-ended. Actually, no harm done...except my shoulder."

"That's why you didn't call?"

"Yes it is...sorry."

"Well, please be careful. Tell your lovely wife I said hello. And David, your driving is really awful!"

Smitty was celebrating his order from Blue Stone. Beer in hand, he pointed to Robert and said, "Thank you for all your help!"

Kelly almost choked, "I didn't know you two were so close?"

"We are now! He was awesome, tracked every detail, meeting, objection and contract exception. I misjudged how talented he is. I'd have him on my account management team anytime."

A sample plan to manage a key account is next. Modify the plan to fit your specific needs! The templates or forms you design can be paper-based or electronic, stand-alone documents or part of a salesforce automation platform. Whichever format you choose, get comfortable—because you are destined to spend quality time creating, editing and reviewing this information.

Each of the illustrations used in The Steps To Managing A Key Account can be found in Appendix C at the back of this book. The Selling Pyramid and Business Sales Methodology are explained in *Smart Selling!* The Competitor's Resume and The Competitor's Profile are detailed in ***Winning Business from Difficult Competitors.***

The Steps To Managing

Identify The Account:

Business Name

Address

Telephone

E-mail

Current Customer or Prospect

Key Executive Contacts

Why Is This A Key Relationship?

What Does The Account Need?

The Proposed Product Or Service:

The Selling Pyramid:

Who We Will Sell To?

What They Need?

The Message To Be Delivered?

THE "Cs"
CEO - CFO

EXECUTIVE BUYERS
EVP - SVP - Group VP

Business Executives with Budget
THE CIO
Technologist Who Recommends

THE RECOMMENDERS
Vice Presidents or Directors
Department - Product - Functional Managers

THE EVALUATORS
Consultants - Project Managers - Technical Specialists
Coaches   Gatekeepers

A Key Account

Business Sales Methodology

What Stage Is Next In
The Sales Process?

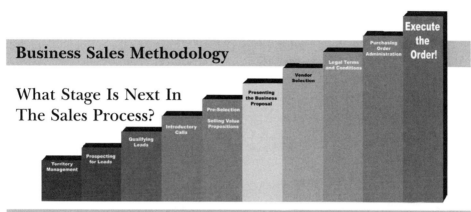

The Strategy To Prevail Against Adversaries:

The Competitor's
Profile

What's The Current Competitive Status?

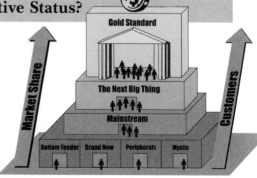

Goals-Actions-Results To Be Accomplished:

By Whom? When?

What's The Plan To Win This Business?

TEST YOUR KNOWLEDGE

1. Sales managers have a fundamental responsibility to lead account management planning sessions and progress reviews.   True/False

2. Account management plans allow you to:
   ❏ Allocate business resources.
   ❏ Plan a strategy for each opportunity.
   ❏ Gather account information.
   ❏ All of the above.

3. What is the ultimate goal of account management?

_____

4. Once you create an account management plan, it's a mistake to begin making changes.   True/False

5. Sales managers need to establish a review process for key accounts.   True/False

6. Sales representatives rarely need a second opinion about the accounts they manage.   True/False

7. Managing key accounts requires leading a team of people. True/False

8. The more a sales manager knows about the accounts his sales team is working, the more he can help.   True/False

9. It's okay for salespeople and their teams to present inconsistent messages to a prospect.   True/False

10. Significant business opportunities deserve the time and effort required to create an account management plan.   True/False

CHAPTER 9

Effective Forecasting

Promise what you can deliver...
and
deliver what you promise!

What is a forecast?

A forecast is a definitive prediction of future sales performance. It applies to individual salespeople and the complete sales team. The forecast is set against a specific date in time, typically the end of a financial reporting period. It is used to project in advance which sales opportunities are ready to move to closure and when that will happen. Forecasting is a primary responsibility for sales managers and is often a difficult challenge.

The larger the business, the more complex the sales forecasting process. Whether your business is large or small, one fact remains constant: An accurate forecast is critical to manage a business effectively...an inaccurate projection of sales performance can be devastating to an organization and to everyone who is part of the enterprise.

The business press is replete with stories about financial executives at public companies complaining that they have little confidence in the forecasts they are receiving from their sales teams. Without this information, even basic financial projections are of questionable value.

Sometimes, you will hear that the projected sales have been lost; on other occasions, the problem is that the opportunities have been delayed. These deferred sales may not be lost completely, but may have slipped into some future month, quarter or year. The problem is not unique to public enterprises; it impacts millions of private companies all across the business spectrum.

Let's look for a moment at some of the key business challenges forecasting impacts:
- Support for new customers
- Inventory and raw material requirements
- Staffing requirements to manufacture, deliver and support the product
- Facility planning
- Cash flow requirements
- Profits
- Planning for the future direction of the enterprise

I'm sure you could add other issues to this list! Misjudging any one of these subjects can severely damage a business; collectively, they are lethal. Companies of all sizes and financial resources have failed because they misunderstood their sales opportunities.

Despite all the discussions and hand-wringing about the need for accurate forecasts, in my opinion, the intellect, discipline and methodology to improve how well sales managers individually and collectively forecast continues to languish. That does not mean forecasting is easy to improve or that there is a magic algorithm that can be applied to make this challenge disappear, but....

Let me sum it up with a piece of common wisdom:

You can make it happen!
You can watch it happen!
or
You can continue to wonder what the hell happened!

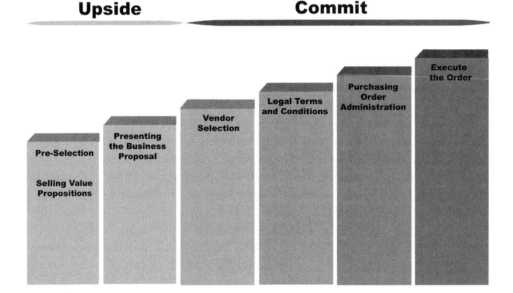

How can you create accurate forecasts?

All forecasting starts with individual salespeople and rolls up through whatever organizational hierarchy you have collectively embraced. Forecasting is not a top-down exercise.

The first order is to focus on the importance of creating accurate forecasting. Executive management and the VP of sales have to promote the important role forecasting plays in the operation of the company. Individual sales representatives have to embrace its value on a personal and business level, and commit to working toward the accurate disclosure a successful business requires. Every business–no matter how small or how modest the expectations–needs to forecast sales results.

Second, you need a culture that promotes and rewards accurate disclosure. The trap often faced in achieving accurate disclosure is both complex and adversarial. It works like this:

When your sales team achieves plan, there is often little emphasis or interest in exploring how plan was reached! You justifiably celebrate the accomplishment and move on. What people fail to examine is, *"Did we close the opportunities we projected? If not, why not? Were there surprise closes, and why did we miss them in our original projection?"*

When results disappoint, group and individual interrogations begin! *"How could this happen, who is to blame for this? This better not happen again!"* If this sounds all too familiar, it's because it takes place in businesses on a regular basis, big and small, simple and sophisticated.

The signal sent to the sales staff from these actions suggests that the smart approach to forecasting is to promise nothing—that way if they do deliver a sale, they will be praised. Perhaps, more importantly, they will not be criticized for failing to deliver anything because they avoided making any commitments. Salespeople who continue to produce wildly optimistic forecasts that never materialize are removed or disciplined, which sends a further reinforcing message. Sales managers who allow and validate poor forecasting are eventually judged as poor leaders.

Companies often lack a common sales methodology and common terminology to evaluate a prospect's status. Sales reps add to the challenge of the forecast process by stumbling over verbiage. *"Oh, you thought I meant this account would really close this month! Actually, I didn't promise anything other than my best effort to close it. Unfortunately, the budget is still up in the air!"*

The sales management team is then forced to perform "surgery on the uncooperative patients" in order to extract something approaching acceptable sales projections. Executive management has little confidence in sales forecasts that have shown little or no accurate results, and should not be asked to rely on them!

The financial people begin to factor the projections up or down. In the end, no one is really accountable for anything concrete. The sales management team quickly realizes they are in a lose-lose environment. Executive management distrusts the forecast, and the salespeople resent being forced to make commitments.

A business culture that supports accurate forecasting:
- Values and compensates salespeople for selling the product and services their sales plan requires.
- Values and compensates salespeople for achieving the forecasts they commit to deliver.

Reward sales representatives who understand and deliver accurate forecasts! The reward system can include more lucrative commission arrangements, bonus payments or countless other forms of recognition. Anyone who has managed a team of salespeople, small or large, quickly comes to understand that most sales behavior can be focused with a written sales plan that sets clear and demonstrable rewards for the performance you desire. Accurate forecasting is no more nor less achievable than any other sales challenge if managers make it a point of focus and reinforce it through a compensation plan! In fact, we have enclosed a sample Sales Compensation Plan.

Third, salespeople need to embrace the fact that accurate sales forecasts are important to their personal success. Sales representatives often ask their managers why they should care about forecasts..."*What's in it for me? I don't want to be held accountable for this task! Why go through all the trouble of getting it right?*" I believe there's a simple answer—it will make you money, each week, each month and every quarter!

**Forecasting is a basic part of every sales assignment.
It deserves the best professional effort.**

In my selling career, it took me several years to understand how to break the cycles of "feast or famine". There is a tendency for most salespeople to get several well-qualified prospects and work those opportunities to closure. They focus all their energy and effort on those key opportunities and convince themselves this is the correct action to take. When sales are finalized, they victoriously come up for air only to realize that the pipelines are essentially empty! Now, they are months away from the next real sale. It is a disheartening cycle and essentially means they are starting the selling assignment all over! It is also a point at which many sales people decide to find another job rather than restart the process. In time, you learn the value of continuous prospecting and working a sales methodology with a forecast system that clearly gives you a view of what you have to do to create a predictable revenue stream. This reinforcement reminds you to take the tactical and strategic actions necessary to replenish your pipeline before it runs dry and panic sets in.

Compensating for accurate forecasting adds increased focus to the process. Remember, our goal is accuracy. The rewards are forfeited if you miss the forecast by either exceeding your projection or by failing to reach the projection. As an example, the starting point of this policy may be to say that all salespeople must submit their forecast within x days or weeks of the reporting period. The forecast must be accurate to the 90th percentile for qualification to receive the program bonus. Sales representatives should be expected to explain and defend their forecast as part of this process.

Top sales performers understand that forecasting is essential to the business they own or where they work. Salespeople who view the task of forecasting as creating unnecessary or unappreciated stress need to be reminded that selling is ultimately about delivering results on a projected timetable for all the reasons discussed earlier. It is very easy to lose sight of the impact a forecast has as it rolls up through an organization.

The best of intentions aside, misleading yourself and others with a misguided sales forecast serves no purpose.

Fourth, you need a business sales methodology to create the foundation for a forecast that is accurate. If you do not have a customer-focused methodology for managing your prospects to closure, you have no consistent basis for deciding who is going to close and when. The alternative is your *best intuition* which is not exactly the ideal foundation for successful selling. The sales management team is also exposed trying to consolidate commitments that come from salespeople with disparate definitions of when a particular opportunity will close.

I have attended sales meetings where some sales representatives will forecast the imminent closure of opportunities they have yet to qualify, or meet, based on an intuition. Other salespeople at the same meeting will only forecast business that is in the process of "cutting purchase orders." Getting everyone to work from the same playbook, with a common foundation and terminology, can quickly solve this very common problem.

The Four Simple Rules
for Accurate Forecasting

RULE #1

Forecasts are done on fixed schedules with a standardized format. Everybody with sales responsibility produces a forecast, undertaking the forecasting exercise multiple times during a financial reporting period.

Deciding how frequently a forecast is prepared will be based on the nature of your business. For example, if you sell expensive products or services with long selling cycles, you may want to forecast on a monthly schedule. Products that have shorter sales cycles and are volume-oriented may be projected on a weekly basis or several times each week. You will also be guided by your need to do financial reporting. Public companies are focused on quarterly and annual reporting periods. Many privately owned enterprises do financial reporting monthly, quarterly, and annually. Forecasts should provide guidance for and coincide with your accounting periods.

I have provided a template of a sales forecast that you can tailor to your specific needs. It is essential that all forecasts are done in a standard template so there is no confusion about the individual and group disclosures that are taking place. Nothing is more frustrating than sorting through disparate forms, all of which provide similar but different information while the success of your business hangs in the balance. This is also the same underlying reason that no one with responsibility for sales revenue is exempted from submitting a forecast. You cannot project what you do not know about! What you do not know can and will hurt your business.

Since you will be doing standardized forecasts on a scheduled basis, you will have indications in advance of how your company will perform before the end of any financial reporting period—information that allows you and your business to adjust, respond and manage the impact of positive or negative sales trends. As you progress through your financial reporting period, the forecast should begin to tighten and provide greater clarity of projected performance.

The accounts you are projecting and tracking will have progressed through our *Business Sales Methodology* or will be stalled for various reasons. You will have a more finite sense of how much has to happen for a prospect to become a customer in the forecast time you have remaining.

RULE #2

Accounts that have not entered into pre-selection selling are not eligible to be placed on a forecast!

Evaluate all accounts in the status of pre-selection selling as potential "upsides." These potential opportunities can be brought to closure in a defined forecast period but it would be a stretch to finalize them. The time period is of your choosing: it can be a week, month, quarter or year. The important point is that these accounts, promising but incomplete from a selling prospective, are where you concentrate efforts to cover the potential shortfalls you may discover in your sales projections.

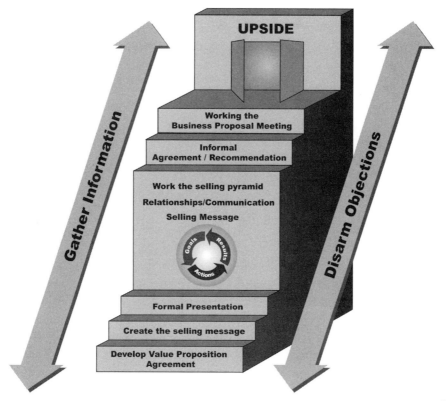

To forecast an account as an "upside" you must:
- Be clearly in pre-selection selling,
- Have reached a mutual agreement on the acceptance of the value proposition,
- Be informally selected by a Recommender in the account,
- Have ongoing dialogue with the Executive Buyer,
- Be progressing to the business proposal meeting.

RULE #3

Your goal is to have enough "commit" accounts to meet or exceed the sales projection toward which you are working. Your experience will guide you to the "overage" in commits you will need to achieve plan safely.

To regard an account as "commit", you must:
- Have been formally notified that you are the selected vendor,
- Have an agreement to execute the order by a specific date, which is within the forecast timeline.
- Have a mutual plan with your prospect to monitor the execution of the order.

RULE #4

"Upside" accounts are fallbacks that are available for replacing "commits" that fail to close on schedule, and become future "commits" as you move forward.

I recommend counting on "upsides" to cover no more than 20 percent of your plan. You should target having three dollars of "upside" prospects to cover each dollar of "commits" that you may be lacking. You can refine these metrics as you gain forecast experience with your specific environment. I frequently hear, "Isn't forecasting supposed to be much more complicated?" The truth is that many organizations have made

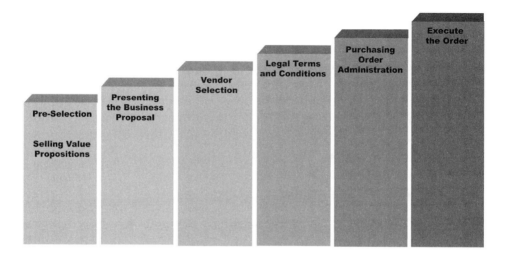

forecasting more complicated than it has to be. At times, companies overreact to a vexing problem by developing complicated account-rating systems, set against a equally complex percentage-to-close factoring formula. A friend observed not long ago, *"How do I forecast 75 percent of a deal? —especially if I only have one opportunity to close! If the opportunity is for $100,000, I am going to deliver either zero or $100,000. I will not deliver $75,000 on the forecast!"*

My advice is, keep the forecasting process simple and get your organization behind it. Once it is up and working well, then begin to refine it; and that may include making it more complicated. Just remember that your goal is accuracy. Complexity is only valuable if it refines accuracy.

A quick review of the components of effective forecasting:

1. **The forecasting discipline must become a point of organizational focus and be part of the sales compensation plan.**

2. **Forecasts are done on fixed schedules with standardized formats. Everyone with sales responsibility participates.**

3. **The *Business Sales Methodology* becomes the forecast template.**

4. **The criteria a prospect must meet to be ultimately forecasted as an "upside" or "commit" are clearly defined.**

101

Value of Accounts

How do I determine the monetary value of the accounts that are forecasted?

It is not uncommon for a forecast to be accurate in predicting which prospects will come to closure in a given timeframe, but to misjudge completely the dollar value of the final sale amount. Welcome to one of the complications of getting an accurate forecast! Salespeople are often challenged by prospects trying to decide not just to purchase the product, but having a multitude of decisions about optional features that may be provided, and ultimately the initial quantity they will order. Everyone wants to sell prospects the maximum amount of product they can be persuaded to order.

- Here are my suggestions for forecasting when you face this challenge: Forecast the minimum order size as a "commit" and "upside" any additional revenue.

- Avoid the temptation to forecast the largest or most optimistic order configuration without fully disclosing the "risk" involved in the transaction. I have seen incredibly optimistic account forecasting turn what was a great order and sales victory into a psychological disappointment due to unrealistic expectations. I have also seen sales lost because sales representatives pushed for order quantities that were unrealistic due to forecasting blunders.

- Discuss your "dilemma" with your prospect and ask for advice. I can assure you it will precipitate a very valuable and mutually informative discussion.

Should the sales forecasting process be automated?

The simple answer to this question is Yes! The complex part of the equation becomes how to apply the many possible forms of technology that are at your disposal in a way that gives you real value. I like to look at technology in this instance as a way to:

1. Accelerate the collection of forecast data,
2. Sort, analyze and track both current and historical forecast data,
3. Quickly distribute the forecast throughout the entire enterprise.

The type or degree of technology you apply should not burden your business by creating more work than value. You may decide that a simple spreadsheet application is sufficient, or that this task requires a sophisticated salesforce automation solution. I have listened to numerous sales representatives and managers express frustration with salesforce automation projects that have become data entry nightmares, and in the end, deliver marginal results that are occasionally referenced by sales, sales management or other company executives. Technology should not be viewed as a way to take business judgment out of forecasting or to replace that organizational responsibility. Instead, it should be seen as a tool, or set of tools, that is flexible enough to make your forecasting methodology efficient, accurate and accessible.

What is the difference between a forecast and a pipeline?
It is easy to confuse these two terms. A **forecast** is composed of upsides and commits, both of which have minimally entered into at least pre-selection in our methodology. A **pipeline** is your forecast, plus accounts that are qualified but not yet in pre-selection. In our methodology these accounts are reflected in the "qualification" and "introductory call" stages. I often refer to these accounts as qualified suspects. Pipelines are useful for watching and analyzing early-stage sales cycle activity.

A note of caution about pipeline activity is in order. Early-stage sales cycle activity is very speculative and can be misleading. Qualifying an account is not a one-time exercise. You constantly re-qualify as you progress through a sales cycle. The simple fact is that early in a sales process you will initially qualify a suspect for your product. That may well qualify the new prospect to be placed in your sales pipeline. Unfortunately, many of these prospects will fall by the wayside as you enter into "introductory calls" and "pre-selection selling."

The real value of pipelines, at an individual and company-wide level, will come from comparing the value of your current data to historical data, and extrapolating trends. Large and robust pipelines should not be viewed as a substitute for closed business, a reason to relax, or an excuse to kick back.

A mentor once observed that individuals and enterprises that were struggling always had large pipelines. He would refer to this phenomenon as 'the curse of an optimistic sales mind speaking to management's happy ears.'

The Pipeline Template

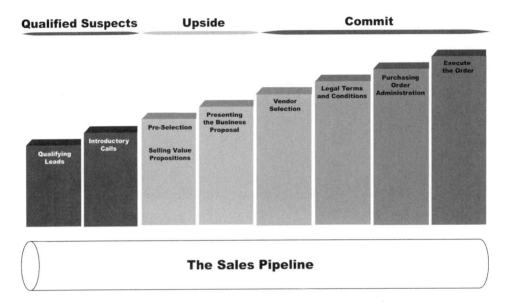

Qualified Suspects   Upside   Commit

The Sales Pipeline

Should I track prospects that have dropped off a forecast?

The answer is Yes! We have provided you with a Lost Prospect Analysis to help you do just that. The value of this exercise is to allow you to analyze both the "upsides" and "commits" that failed to come to closure. At the levels of both an individual sales representative and a company, this information can give you a picture of why business is being lost and how to correct the problem. I encourage you to call the Executive Buyers, Recommenders, and Evaluators at each prospect to get their individual perspective. My own experience is that you will be amazed how freely most people will speak and share information with you. Losing an order is always painful...but losing late in the cycle is both painful and expensive!

Here are just some of the difficult issues you should be probing:
- Was the purchase cancelled or awarded to a competitor? Perhaps the prospect solved their need with an alternative solution that your company did not offer?
- Did your sales team meet the prospect's expectations?
- Was your selling message or value proposition clear, and did the prospect understand the value of your offering?
- Are competitors exploiting a real or a perceived weakness in your company, products or service?
- Are you truly qualifying the prospects? Or are you now discovering

ospects that had never been—really

ve to be the strength and weakness of
tion's solution? Ask the same question
es.

n your company other than the sales-
ions. The final piece of wisdom I will
cussion, you must listen, be sincere in solic-
sive comments or judgmental behavior.

ser," as difficult as it may prove to be,
be greatly diminished. Unfortunately,

bout forecasting

n at any one time; is forecasting real-

small number of prospects you have
to be extraordinarily focused on winning each deal. Forecasting becomes
an important tool in helping you understand all the details of your opportunity. Secondly, forecasting also reminds you that having more than one
opportunity is really paramount to increasing your chances for personal
success. I am always mystified about the one deal at a time question. What
you need to ask is, *"Am I working one deal at a time because I choose to do this, or
is the market for my product imposing this reality on me?"* My experience is that
this is often a self-imposed issue!

I have lots of small deals for which I'm responsible; forecasting seems like too much effort to me!
I would argue that the way to get the most efficient use of your selling
time is to get organized, especially in the environment where you are
working. Forecasting will give you a clear roadmap of which accounts
need your immediate attention, when they need it, and then allow you to
manage them to closure. You also get the benefit of being able to project
your results into the future.

Can I have more "commits" than I need to make my plan? Should I fore-cast being over plan?
You certainly can have more "commits" than you need to make plan; it is
a great problem to have. Just remember that not all your "commits" will

necessarily come to closure and some percentage of your "upsides" may close. I would not hesitate to forecast being over plan; just remember to use your best judgment, and make the forecast as accurate as you can. In a moment of euphoria, do not make the mistake of setting expectations on which you cannot deliver.

Should I ever forecast missing plan?
This is always a difficult position to be in. The answer is simple: disclose reality. The only thing worse than missing plan is misleading yourself and others by forecasting things that are not going to happen. Use this setback to develop a plan to move your prospects to closure for the next reporting period.

It appears to me that whenever I do a forecast, the inquisition from my manager begins! Am I missing something?
Twenty-five plus years of sales experience has taught me that one person's idea of an inquisition may be another's image of a fireside chat. That aside, there are several reasons that you should be doing a forecast, even if it's only for your own benefit. First, you will get a clear picture of how your current sales efforts are paying off, and what *Goals-Actions-Results* need to come next as you manage your key prospects to closure. Sales professionals realize their businesses need forecasts to survive and prosper. They understand that creating accurate forecasts is a win-win. I will also wager you that the more accurate your forecasts become, the less unpleasant the inquisitions will become.

What do I do with sales representatives who just refuse to cooperate in doing a forecast or who claim the exercise costs them valuable selling time!
This is a common challenge sales management faces. It is also why I suggest tying forecasting to sales compensation plans. If you take this action, a failure to forecast or to do it accurately will cost your salespeople money. That is not something they will ignore. At a deeper level, you will need to reinforce that forecasting is important to your business and their ability to achieve personal success. In my experience, most salespeople who ignore forecasting do it because you allow it to happen, or they fear being held accountable. Both situations need to be addressed whatever the circumstances.

Our collective "commits" and "upsides" really do not come close to my business plan. Where does that leave my company?
The value of a forecast is that it prepares you for reality and gives you an opportunity to make adjustments. You can either take extraordinary

actions to move prospects through the steps in our sales methodology or you can disclose, rethink and revise both your sales and business plans.

We do not seem to have an organized system of forecasting, and yet we spend enormous amounts of time in meetings about making plan. Any suggestions?
Start your next meeting by spending an hour as a group reviewing this chapter. I suspect you can quickly agree to implement our forecasting methodology.

Effective forecasting has three core audiences: Business Executives, Sales Managers and Salespeople.

Executives need the fundamental business knowledge that comes from accurate and timely forecasts. Sales Managers need a clear target list of prospects for closure, time to act to persuade those prospects, and a picture of individual sales performance. Salespeople need forecasts as a self-generated report card of their work efforts and a path to financial success.

> **Forecasting is difficult and, in many cases, painful, because it forces one to face reality, pleasant or not, and then to act on that reality. The difficulty applies in equal measure to business executives, managers, and sales representatives. Forecasting emphasizes that a disorganized selling effort reverberates throughout the business and has a far-reaching impact.**

The approach to effective forecasting I have suggested can and will improve the accuracy of your sales projections. The technique is systematic and provides common terms and foundations everyone can use. It is integrated with a concrete sales methodology. It will not burden your organization with meaningless complexity. The incentives for rewarding accurate disclosure can quickly be incorporated in your sales commission or compensation plans.

Accurate forecasting is driven from the bottom up in an organization. The forms provided in the workbook allow you to forecast, consolidate and examine lost opportunities at an individual and enterprise-wide level.

A commitment to insisting upon accurate forecasting is a priority every sales manager needs to undertake. The issue is too important both to you and your organization for anything short of your full attention!

Norton was about to make his initial presentation to the executive committee of Baker Industries. He realized this was his first opportunity since joining the company to intermingle with the executives he hoped would soon be his peers. His ambitions reached far beyond the VP of Sales assignment, but for now it would serve as a convenient starting point. His time at AG International had allowed him to develop significant experience at conducting important executive briefings. AG was a dominant player in the marketplace with Baker as the acknowledged runner-up. Perhaps the trading down experience clouded his judgment. He would admit to friends his experience at Baker—waiting for Al's imminent departure—was neither interesting nor particularly challenging. In fact, he begun to regret having accepted his current diminished sales role. He had lost his edge...and misjudged the focus his new company placed on forecasting.

Daniel Kelly, the CEO, looked tired and jaundiced. Norton was struck by the noticeable physical change in just six short months. The room was packed with senior executives, managers, accountants and various administrative assistants. Several important directors and legal advisors were also in attendance.

Kelly reviewed several strategic goals the company had set and reported on the measured results of the initiatives. "The final goal for this fiscal year is financial...we must grow sales by 3%. I'm worried about our progress and our salesforce's execution. Al and Norton will take us through their forecast and whatever adjustments they are planning to execute to insure we reach our objective."

Al's presentation was brief and straight to the point. "We have two sales teams each with about 25 salespeople. Karen's group is at plan and should finish right on target. Robert is at 70% of plan and is struggling. I want to clear the air about his performance–I have to take responsibility for promoting him prematurely. I believe he will become an outstanding manager, but he is in over his head and it's my fault. Norton has rolled up his sleeves and is working day to day with Robert's team. We have a long way to go to make plan and I must tell you I believe that despite our best efforts we are going to fall short."

The audience stirred and someone asked; "How short...is short?"

"About 5% short. Norton is up next, he will take you through all of the details."

The accountants were already re-running their numbers.

Norton strode to the podium. This was his moment to shine and he fully intended to bask in his new found importance.

"I spent five years at AG International as VP of Sales so this is very familiar territory. I made my numbers every year; and every year, someone said it could not be done! I am an optimist and with your help

108

I can deliver plan."

The room was buzzing...The new guy had contradicted Al...he did it openly and without any hesitation. Part of the audience was relieved to hear there was no problem, the others knew the problem was worse than they had anticipated. The CFO whispered to Daniel, "We have a numbers problem and a leadership problem!"

Daniel, trying to recover his composure, turned his full attention to Norton. "Very interesting...could you take us through your detailed forecast...so we can get a sense of your optimism?"

Al exited the room to cold stares, he was in search of Karen and Robert. He found Bob Kelly first.

"I need Karen and Robert in my office. Norton is upstairs committing suicide in front of your brother!"

Bob knew panic when he saw it, his first reaction was to do as asked, but he decided first to calm Al Winters down. "Boss, let's not have a stroke...start at the beginning and tell me what happened. I'm paging Karen's cell phone right now."

Winters caught his breath and composure as Karen entered the room. "Personal issues aside, Norton is about to assure people he is going to solve a problem he can't solve! We all know the forecast is short. Why would he do this?"

Karen caught Al's stare, "Because he is Norton being Norton. It's just how he is. Team is not in his vocabulary."

Winter's administrative assistant stuck his head into the room, "They want you back upstairs...right away! They're also asking for Bob, Karen and Robert."

Norton was trapped as he attempted to deliver the forecast details. Robert's team had little documentation to support their numbers and several variations of how they projected sales. Some accounts were factored, others were not, the weighing percentages were all different. The terms and forms in use varied from salesperson to salesperson. Norton's papers were being shuffled and reshuffled. What jumped out at the audience was confusion! The tense environment was only heightened by the now obvious state of his confusion.

The VP of Marketing commented, "How can you possibly expect us to buy into your assurances when we can't even make sense of this mess of a forecast! I can't figure out how you can manage with this information, let alone assure us everything will be fine. You are really making me nervous."

A financial analyst chided Norton, "You missed the forecast you submitted last quarter by 15%, right?...you do remember?"

The comments and skepticism continued.

"How can you make up this shortfall while you have three unfilled sales positions?"

"Look, you can't expect a forecast to be black and white. I am not used to having my word questioned, and I don't particularly appreciate your insinuations!"

The CEO ended the skirmish with a clear statement. "Norton, I don't know what your last remark means; but I can assure you, we take forecasting very seriously around here and expect the projections to be clear and accurate!"

Karen entered the room at just that moment. Daniel Kelly turned to her in exasperation, "Tell me you have a forecast someone can make sense of?"

Momentarily stunned, Karen regained her composure. "I can give you a complete projection for my team. If you want details, I can certainly oblige you, I will just need about 15 minutes to get set up."

The meeting was quickly recessed. Norton left the room with no intention of returning.

"I need to start by taking you through the methodology I use..."

The room erupted into laughs and snickering. The CFO stood up. "Did you say methodology? meaning a standard? Thank goodness at last some sanity! Please..."

"The business sales methodology on the screen is integrated into our forecasting. 'Upsides' are in pre-selection selling, and 'Commits' are triggered by the prospect's formal selection of our business proposal. The next screen gives you the formal definition of both terms. We all work under four basic forecast rules which are now in front of you. Questions?"

"Do you weigh or factor each deal?"

"No, not as a sales team. The deals are upside or commit. We expect each salesperson to make plan with their commit accounts. Shortfalls up to 20% can be covered by upside accounts."

"The approach looks very straightforward."

"Its strength is in being clean and simple. Once you get the definitions and a few basic rules down, the complexity of forecasting is reduced." Karen went through the commits and upsides during the next two hours, answering questions, jotting suggestions down and noting unanswered questions about each account.

Daniel began to push on her final projections.

"Why can't you do better than the 105% of plan you're forecasting? It looks to me as if you can. Is your team motivated or what?"

"I don't want to create expectations I can't achieve. This team has never achieved 105% of its annual plan...ever...not once in the last five years."

"Fine, but this is an extraordinary circumstance. You do realize that, right?"

She was starting to hesitate when...

Bob Kelly got up and slowly walked to the front of the room. His presence broke the conversation. He handed Karen a neatly folded note.

Someone asked, "What's he doing?"

His quick humor bit into the audience, "Hey, when your younger brother is CEO you get to stretch your legs and deliver an occasional important message to a friend!"

Karen glanced at the note. It contained a familiar phrase: *"Promise what you can deliver...and deliver what you promise! Never a penny more!"* She set her jaw and nodded at Bob.

Daniel glared at his brother, muttered to himself, and ended the pointed questioning...for now.

The TV was blaring, Bob was about done with the 10 o'clock news and ready for bed. His son handed him the phone. "It's Uncle Dan, he say's to tell you it's an emergency."

"Bob, before you say a word...just get in the car and drive over here. I'm not going to sleep until we get this fixed."

"I'm in my PJ's."

"So what, just get over here!"

"Okay, 15 minutes...but just one question, are you still enjoying your job?"

The line was already dead.

TEST YOUR KNOWLEDGE

1. An accurate forecast is critical to manage a business effectively.

   True/False

2. Salespeople need to embrace the fact that accurate sales forecasts are important to their personal success.   True/False

3. Define both the terms "Upside" and "Commit".

   ....

   ....

   ....

4. What is the difference between a Pipeline and a Forecast?

   ....

   ....

   ....

5. Building your forecast from a sales methodology will cause confusion that you can easily avoid.   True/False

6. List The Four Simple Rules for Accurate Forecasting:

   1. ....

   2. ....

   3. ....

   4. ....

7. Name several important reasons to track "lost prospects" from your pipeline: ....

   ....

   ....

8. What are some negative ramifications a business will face with an inaccurate forecast? ....

   ....

Effective Forecasting

WORKBOOK

Forms

Workbook Instructions:

Sales Forecast Forms

We have provided you with three levels of Forecast forms, each designed to roll up to the next reporting level.

    1. An Individual Prospect Forecast

    2. A Sales Representative Forecast

    3. A Consolidated Forecast

Pipeline Forms

We have provided for two levels of Pipeline disclosure information.

    1. Sales Representative Pipeline

    2. Consolidated Pipeline

Lost Prospect Analysis

We encourage you to use this form and its questions to start your examination of lost sales opportunities. You may want to modify and customize the questions as you gain experience with the discovery process.

Sales Compensation Plan

This sample plan is provided to remind you of the necessity of having written sales plans. It also integrates the sample rewards for accurate and timely forecasting.

Upside/Commit Definitions

A handy reference guide to the requirements for forecasting an Upside or Commit account

Notice: The forms included with this publication are proprietary and have been provided for the exclusive use of Business Skills Press LLC. customers and their employees. The forms may not be resold or distributed without our expressed written consent.

Prospect Forecast

©2007 Business Skills Press LLC

Date:	Sales Rep:	Business Unit:	Forecasting Period:

Prospect Name:

Product:

Name:

Key Prospect Contact(s):
- ☐ CEO/CFO
- ☐ Executive Buyer
- ☐ CIO
- ☐ Recommender
- ☐ Evaluator

THE "Cs"
CEO · CFO

EXECUTIVE BUYERS
EVP · SVP · Group VP

Business Executives with Budget
THE CIO
Technologist Who Recommends

THE RECOMMENDERS
Vice Presidents or Directors
Department · Product · Functional Managers

THE EVALUATORS
Consultants · Project Managers · Technical Specialists
Coaches · Gatekeepers

Upside   Commit

Selling Value Propositions
Pre-Selection

Presenting the Business Proposal

Vendor Selection

Legal Terms and Conditions

Purchasing Order Administration

Execute the Order

Current Status

Current Account Status:

☐ Upside
☐ Commit

Value of Sale:

Next Step

Next step in Methodology:

Date to be accomplished: ____/____/____   Estimated date of final execution: ____/____/____

Assistance Required:

115

Sales Representative Forecast

Date: ....

Sales Rep: ....

Business Unit: ....

Forecasting Period: ....

Upside

Commit

| Pre-Selection | Presenting the Business Proposal | Vendor Selection | Legal Terms and Conditions | Purchasing Order Administration | Execute the Order |
| Selling Value Propositions | | | | | |

Amount per category

Forecast per prospect

Prospects

Forecasts per category

Total Forecast ....

Consolidated Forecast

Date:	Sales Rep:	Business Unit:	Forecasting Period:

Upside | **Commit**

Pre-Selection	Presenting the Business Proposal	Vendor Selection	Legal Terms and Conditions	Purchasing Order Administration	Execute the Order

Selling Value Propositions

Forecasts per sales rep

Amount per category

Sales Representatives

Consolidated Forecast

Forecasts per category

Sales Representative Pipeline

©2007 Business Skills Press LLC

Date: ....

Sales Rep: ....

Business Unit: ....

Forecasting Period: ....

Qualified Suspects

Upside

Commit

Qualifying Leads

Introductory Calls

Pre-Selection

Selling Value Propositions

Presenting the Business Proposal

Vendor Selection

Legal Terms and Conditions

Purchasing Order Administration

Execute the Order

Forecasts per prospect

Amount per category

Prospects

Forecasts per category

Consolidated Pipeline

©2007 Business Skills Press LLC

Date: ....

Business Unit: ....

Forecasting Period: ....

Qualified Suspects	Upside	Commit

Qualifying Leads	Introductory Calls	Pre-Selection	Selling Value Propositions	Presenting the Business Proposal	Vendor Selection	Legal Terms and Conditions	Purchasing Order Administration	Execute the Order

Sales Representatives

Amount per category

Forecasts per Representative

Forecasts per category

Total Consolidated Pipeline ....

119

Lost Prospect Analysis

Date:	Prospect Name:	Sales Rep:	Interviewed by:

Prospect

Title

Contact info:

Position in Selling Pyramid:
- ☐ CEO/CFO
- ☐ Executive Buyer
- ☐ CIO
- ☐ Recommender
- ☐ Evaluator

Why were we eliminated:
- ☐ Planned Purchase was canceled
  - Why?
- ☐ Elected to solve the "need" in a different way.
  - How?
- ☐ Selected a competitor. Who?

The Interview

Questions: Did we....

Answers

Rating
1 2 3 4 5

Sales Team
- Listen to your Business Challenges?
- Understand your need?
- Present our solution?
- Explain our Value Proposition?
- Other?

Product Solution
- Explain our F/F/B?
- Meet your requirements?
- Perform Demonstrations?
- Present References?
- Other?

Company
- Explain our Business Mission?
- Introduce our Executive Management?
- Discuss our Cust. Support and Service ?
- Other?

Share with us what you perceive as the strengths/weaknesses of our competitor and ourselves:

(continue on backside)

Sales Compensation Plan
XYZ Company

Date:

Calendar Period of This Plan:

Sales Representative:

Sales Assignment/Territory:

Authorized Products/Service to be sold:

Quota Assigned: $000,000. per annum

   Prorated monthly and quarterly

Target Annual Income:

   Base Salary:

   Commissions at Plan:

   Bonus at Plan:

Commission and Bonus Plan:
- 2% on the amount of all sales up to your assigned quota.
- 3% on the amount of all sales after you have exceeded your annual plan.
- $1,000 p.a. bonus for timely submission of all required monthly forecasts. All forecasts are due the last business day of each month. Bonus is payable quarterly.
- $1,000 p.a. bonus for accurate forecasting. The achievement of 90% of your forecasted sales performance is required. The VP Sales may approve the payment of this bonus, if you exceed both your forecast and plan.

Sales Plan Terms and Conditions:
- Sales will be eligible for booking credit and commission payment when....
- How and when you get paid commission...
- Adherence to ethical business practices and policies....

Legal Obligations and Disclosures:
- How your employment status can affect commission payments...
- This plan is/is not a binding contractual agreement....
- Disputes are resolved by.....
- We reserve the right to make revisions to this plan....

Date Executed: _____

_____   _____
Company   Sales Representative

Upside/Commit Definitions

Upside Accounts Must:

1. Be clearly in pre-selection selling,
2. Have reached a mutual agreement on the acceptance of the value proposition,
3. Be informally selected by a "Recommender" in the account,
4. Have an ongoing dialogue with the "Executive Buyer",
5. Be progressing to the business proposal meeting.

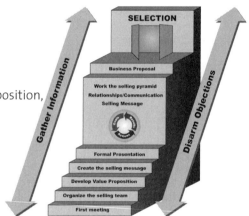

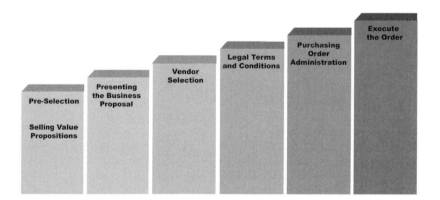

Commit Accounts Must:

1. Have formal notification that we are the selected vendor,
2. Have an agreement to execute the order by a specific date, which is within our forecast timeline,
3. Have a mutual plan to monitor the execution of the order.

The Management And Creation Of Budgets

Every sales manager will have responsibility for the financial plan of their business unit or department. The scope and complexity of the budgets they manage will differ with each assignment and business. Some sales managers may have only expense budgets, others may be held accountable for full profit and loss statements.

I managed sales organizations where budgets were sacred documents, and others which required change-tracking software to keep current with the ongoing revisions. Our discussions in this chapter are not going to focus on accounting principles or standards. Rather, we will focus on the value the budgeting exercise presents to sales managers and the all-too-common pitfalls associated with budgets.

What's the purpose of a budget?
In the simplest of terms, budgets encourage you to create both a plan and a sales strategy for a specific period of time. How can I best deliver the sales targets I must achieve? How should I spend capital to generate sales?

Budgets require managers to make conscious business choices. How many people can I hire, what should they be paid? What marketing programs will I fund? Who will we target for product offers, in what frequency and channel? The scope of these questions and decisions can be endless! If done correctly, the exercise will help you rationalize the potential choices. You will discover whether a proposal to open a new sales channel or re-allocate support resources is a great business opportunity or simply beyond your ability to finance.

The point I want to impress upon you is: Budgets are built around numbers, but the real value is in the thought process and decisions that drive those numbers. The budget is a financial depiction of your specific business plan for the sales organization! The numbers have a diminished value without an underlying plan.

Documents passed down from year to year—periodically adjusted up or down by a few percentage points in an effort to fit a broader financial objective—simply miss the real goal of budgeting.

Sales managers and teams who first plot sales strategy and then decide how to fund their plans have grasped the concept behind budgeting. Conversely, those managers who start with last year's budget and tinker with adjustments to the numbers, really have missed the big picture and opportunity.

124

Creating the budget

Start with your plan! How are you going to sell and market product or services? The sales revenue piece of the equation comes first. Why? A business does not exist without sales. Once you have settled on your revenue plan you can then create the expense budget needed to support it. What will you spend to generate your projected sales?

At this stage, the inevitable adjustment and reconciliation process begins. You now have a projection of sales and expenses and a snapshot of your profit or loss picture. Are you going to make money? Lose money? Revenue shortfalls are balanced by reducing expenses or using capital to cover your losses. You have to weigh whether a reduced cost structure also reduces your ability to sell product.

Budgets are always compromises determined by what you want to do, what you can realistically deliver and how much capital you are able to invest. The ultimate challenge is getting the greatest sales return possible from the capital you have available.

I refer to budgets as living documents. For many businesses, they are constantly being adjusted and realigned. They reflect the reality of uncertain markets for product, economic changes and events beyond your control, experience or imagination. For example, the events of September 11, 2001 had real consequences on the airline and tourism industries. The business environment faced by countless players in these transportation-oriented markets changed in one fateful day. Far less dramatic changes occur each business day, but the effects nonetheless ripple through businesses and their budgets. Revising budgets is a normal response to the change; in fact, failing to adjust budgets can quickly render the documents obsolete and useless.

The more experience you have with developing plans and creating budgets, the greater accuracy you will achieve. In time, you will develop historical knowledge of a product's revenue pattern. New business ventures and product offerings often require several business cycles to tune their accuracy. Enterprises with stable business models have better chances of getting their budgeting exercises very accurate.

Budgets should be open exercises!

Don't lock yourself in a conference room and undertake the task without serious input from your sales team. The best way to get buy-in and commitment is to get salespeople involved and invested in the process and the finished plan. What do your top sales performers feel they can accomplish next year? Why?

The more team-oriented the planning and budgeting process, the greater the collective wisdom you bring to the table. Sales managers often have to make the final call on specific ideas or suggestions, but the participation is vital in itself!

The problem with creating budgets in a vacuum is played out in coffee room conversations each day. "I never agreed to this! Who made this decision? Just ignore it!" A fitting summation of top-down budget exercises.

Perhaps even more disturbing is organizational behavior which begins to engage in poor business practices to accommodate bad budgeting. I cited earlier in the book a dispute in my own career about salespeople and telephone expenses. Telling your team to stop prospecting for leads because the telephone budget has been overrun is not a good business strategy. Preventing a field salesperson from making sales calls because a travel budget problem exists will not get you the results you really want!

Monitoring the budget
One of the truly valuable results of working with a well-planned and constructed budget is the ability to watch for and adjust to trends. A mentor used to constantly stress: "The numbers tell a story, your job is to read the story and decide if you like its ending." The quicker you see the plot unfolding, the better! Budgets will present a picture of how well your sales strategy and plans are working—which is why sales managers devote time to reviewing their numbers frequently. It's not because they are enamored with the numbers per se, but the underlying story they reveal is paramount!

If you are not comfortable with basic accounting or the concepts behind balance sheets and income and expense statements, find a financial person who can help you.

Learning from past budgeting exercises
I always found it helpful to examine a past budget to see how accurate it was and why. What lessons about the sales team's organization, performance and general spending habits did the documents reveal? If travel costs were much higher than anticipated, what was the underlying cause?

Some organizations are excellent in managing expenses, but do poorly when projecting sales revenue. Why? Explore the optimism or misguided expectations and then raise a cautionary flag for the next budget exercise. If you have missed sales projects for the last three years by 20%, before you project yet another 20% increase, stop and think about the assumptions you are embracing!

Are you responsible and accountable for the budget?

Budgets are, unfortunately, often viewed suspiciously because of a disconnect about a fundamental managerial principle...responsibility and accountability.

Managers who have the authority to literally 'write checks' or 'issue commitments' on their budgets are both responsible and accountable. They can act and are judged by the results of their decisions. Simple, elegant and fair! All too many managers are held at peril! They are alleged to be accountable for their budgets but lack the authority to take any action without the approval of someone else or a committee.

> *I can clearly recall being criticized in my first sales management assignment for being over budget. My sales commissions expenses were in excess of the planned levels of expenditure. My recollection of the conversation is still clear:*
> *"Tom, you are way over the budget for commissions!"*
> *"Really...you do realize I am at 150% of the revenue plan?"*
> *"I am only addressing expenses!"*
> *(This was the first tip-off that a disconnect existed.)*
> *"Okay, so you want me to cut staff and reduce commission payments?"*
> *"No, those decisions are way beyond your authority or mine."*
> *(The message was now clear, 'I want to blame you for something you have no control over.')*
> *"I'm missing your point, but...I just want to remind you the headcount was here when I took this assignment, as was the commission plan and the budget."*
> *"So...?"*
> *"So, unfortunately, I am out of time for this meeting! If you want me to take any action, you had best let me know, otherwise I am going to just carry on with selling product!"*

The issue was never raised again and, yes, some would say I was difficult to manage. I would prefer to say that I refused to be drawn into being held accountable for budgets beyond my responsibility—the same advice I will offer to you.

Well-run businesses and those who manage these organizations understand that responsibility and accountability go hand-in-hand. Don't attempt to hold people accountable for budgets they have no ability to manage.

▶ Sunday evening...Karen and the sales team marveled at how quickly the weekend had disappeared. The budget for the next fiscal year was now in draft stage...

The agenda had begun on Friday evening with a kick-off session. Al Winters presented several key points for the benefit of the audience.

"First priority is to rethink how we sell, wipe the slate clean and start from scratch. Once you decide on the best way to approach our prospects and customers, then build an organization, territory plans and finally your revenue plan. Marketing will help with questions about products, promotions, pricing and positioning. Your input will really drive their own strategy for next year! The financial staff is here to assist in running numbers, fleshing out the impact of your decisions and offering guidance. The sales projections you come up with will be taken forward and integrated into a broader planning exercise for the business. Questions?"

"Any guidance on the number you want to see?"

"The numbers I want to see are the numbers you are willing to bet our future on...and yours!"

"Are you in charge of this, Al?"

"No, Karen will run this off-site. I will not be in attendance beyond this evening."

"Are we doing just revenue projections?"

"No, you are also doing a full expense pro-forma. Monday is a holiday so you have the option of staying an extra day if needed."

Karen thanked Al for his generous offer, and called the meeting to order. She led a discussion of this year's budget with current year-to-date performance for each income and expense item.

"As you can see, the revenue is behind plan by 8%, offset in part by lower commissions and a 5% under-run of expenses. We need a strong finish to make plan...which we will do!"

The VP of Marketing reviewed the latest in market data and competitive information.

Sydney updated the anxious group on the progress of the new SC6000 press and, to everyone's delight, pronounced it ready for full release and production at the start of the new business calendar.

Saturday morning, Tad Smith led off the agenda. Smitty was in his 20th year as a sales executive at Baker. The company's first salesperson, he was hired by his friend and mentor Bob Kelly. He never wavered in his refusal to enter the ranks of management. Smitty considered sales a true labor of love and always reminded his co-workers..."This is better than working for a living."

Appearing more as a college professor than a battle-hardened salesperson, his assignment was to propose a new sales model. "We start by building a distributor-centric sales organization in the international markets and expanding the 'team' concept in our domestic territories! Both actions give us the opportunity for substantial revenue growth."

Smitty was rolling along with his explanation, "The SC6000 is a perfect replacement for our older units. Focus our new salespeople on the replacement business, protecting our base and getting experience. Let the senior sales staff finish off AG in the domestic market. We beat AG just over 60% of the time when we compete; but if you take the statistics from our 10 senior reps, that ratio goes up to 85%. It's time to finish AG off!"

In the audience, the financial guys were already cranking numbers. The CFO asked, "What's the comp plan for the junior partner on the team look like? How many hires do you envision, Smitty?" The meeting was off to a fast start.

Smitty was after the distributor proposal next. "We have little or no European presence; we have ceded this market...their home turf...to AG. We need to get our toe in the water. Distributors are a cost effective alternative to setting up a new field sales organization. Any sales we make in this market represent net new growth. Heck, we have six ex-AG employees, several of whom have sold for them in the European theater, and one was a sales manager. Karen covered the UK for 2 years! Let's use our expertise to build a distributor channel!"

Kelly and the CFO left the room for a side conversation. The CFO returned and offered, "I have some consulting money from this year leftover, I could stake Karen $50K to start exploring the opportunity."

"Before we take AG on in Europe, we may want to try the Far East. They're not doing anything much there. Perhaps Karen may want to think about that alternative. New market for both of us. India has a lot of new publishers...just a thought..."

With that, Kelly disappeared again. The marketing folks were already dialing up new research material on foreign industry segments. By 10 p.m. Saturday evening, the first cut of the revenue plan was ready for a Sunday morning review.

The afternoon finished with a heated discussion about pricing and discounting policy. The VP of Marketing pressed for price increases, but the sales team refused to concede the change would result in increased revenue. A reduction in the average sales discounts from 10% to 5% was instead viewed as a better solution to the revenue growth equation.

After dinner, the sales compensation strategy for next year was debated, as well as the restructure of territorial assignments. The arguments were forceful for better pay and lower quotas...and compromises were struck. Base salaries were unchanged, but the incentives for exceeding quota were increased substantially. The teaming proposal eliminated most territorial adjustments and a few new rules for splits of commission were finalized.

"Looks like a nice Fall Sunday...too bad we are all going to spend the day inside."

Without delay, the CFO presented a first-cut revenue pro forma. "Sales growth of 5-8%. Darn good starting point...let's review the assumptions you have put forth."

The discussion went through unit projections by quarter, the pricing model, discount policy and sales headcount. By late morning, the focus shifted to the expense ledger.

A consensus on sales compensation and headcount was already in place, so the numbers came together quickly. Travel costs, entertainment budgets, and communications budgets sparked a lively debate. The new automobile policy was challenged...but survived without revision!

The chief accountant set the tone with her opening statement, "The truth is Baker has a long history of being frugal, that's not about to change. I intend to squeeze every nickel like never before!"

"Well, what is about to change is our build out of a new sales and customer tracking system by this team...that's a must have...right away!"

"There isn't money for any more expansion of your sales administration function or its systems. We have invested quite enough in that project!"

Karen exploded, pointing directly at her antagonist, "That's your opinion! and I refuse to accept either the answer or your attitude!"

Smitty and Kelly winced. "Is she tough as nails when you push her or what?"

"She knows what she wants, Bob. Can't fault her for that!"
A glance and nod from Kelly sent the CFO to his feet.

"Okay...Okay, we'll find the money for the system you want. Let's take a break and all get some air, okay?"

"No. When will you find the money and how much?"

"Karen, you have my word, it will get top priority...please!"

Kelly and the CFO stood outside and exhaled.

"Sorry, Bob, our new accountant is a little rough around the edges."

"I can't afford to push Karen too far, the sales budgets aside, she get's what she wants, unless I specifically say no deal."

"I understand, there will not be a problem!"

Smitty and Karen took a brisk tour of the parking lot.

"Hey, you're almost done with this budget. Don't lose control of the meeting now...relax!"

"Darn annoying."

"The thing about budgets is they're always a balancing act. You plan, compromise, and then make adjustments because things change and new priorities pop-up. The plan you have is well-thought out and constructed. It has the full support of your team."

"I guess so...I wish I could be certain it will work."

"Can't help you with that one. I guess that's why I never wanted to be a sales manager!"

TEST YOUR KNOWLEDGE

1. Every sales manager will have responsibility for a budget.   True/False

2. Budgets are ―――――――――― & ――――――――――
   ❏ Financial plans created by thoughtful business decisions.
   ❏ Static documents that should not be revised.
   ❏ Financial projections of your sales strategy and tactical plans.
   ❏ The responsibility of executive management.

3. Managers who start with last year's budget, then tinker with adjustments, have missed the big picture and opportunity.   True/False

4. Sales managers must have broad participation from their sales team
   to make a budget exercise valuable and binding.   True/False

5. The problem with budgets is they don't tell you how well your
   sales plan is working.   True/False

6. There is little to be learned from reviewing your organization's
   past budgets and supporting documents.   True/False

7. It's reasonable to hold executives accountable for budgets they
   are prohibited from managing.   True/False

8. Budgets are always compromises between what you want to do,
   what you can realistically deliver, and your financial resources.
   True/False

9. Budgets are built around numbers, but the real value is the thought
   process and decisions that drive those numbers.   True/False

10. Poor business practices can result from misguided attempts to
    accommodate budgeting mistakes.   True/False

CHAPTER 11

Evaluating Salespeople

Sales managers create teams by evaluating people and the skills they bring to the organization. Every sales manager will spend a significant amount of time and energy thinking about the consequences of selecting the right people to accomplish important assignments. How well you recruit and train staff, decide when it's appropriate to terminate salespeople and manage resignations will have an immense impact on your success.

Although the statement which follows may seem to be blatantly obvious, it represents the stark reality faced by countless sales managers.

You will not achieve your sales plans when you are understaffed, dependent on poorly trained employees and forced to rely on a team beset with poorly qualified salespeople.

Well-made people decisions will quickly deliver positive results and create exceptional long-term benefits. The people you select for your team will have an immeasurable impact on your business achievements and sales management career which is why it is so important to make good people choices!

Recruiting Salespeople

Hiring top sales performers should be the ultimate goal of each and every recruitment effort you undertake. What is a top performer?

Recruitment mistakes are, unfortunately, difficult to avoid. Making judgments about people, their abilities, motivation, and commitment to excel as sales professionals...are a challenge! To add to the degree of difficulty, you are judging both present and future skill sets and attitudes. The very best sales managers diligently attempt to limit their miscalculations. They recognize when they make the inevitable mistakes—resolution has to quickly follow.

Recruiting a sales representative requires an appetite for risk...Why? Top performers are hard to find and have the ability to choose from lots of opportunities, mediocre practitioners are more plentiful and the inexperienced are always present with limited options and risk-fraught projections of future performance. Welcome to the world of sales recruitment!

Learning to be an effective recruiter is important because sales teams in general are in a constant state of staff turnover. People leave for new opportunities and challenges, personal issues take a toll, some salespeople fail and move on to other occupations. Top performers have a way of getting promotions and landing new assignments, perhaps in your company or somewhere else!

The industry, markets and business you are part of will all have different turnover experience. Fortunate sales managers may replace 20% of their staff each year, others will replace 100% or more on an annual basis. Every sales manager wants to limit their staff losses, and the best managers will clearly have lower turnover rates. This issue challenges everyone!

We are going to spend our limited time discussing where to find future top performers, how to best qualify them, what is required to recruit salesmen and women professionally, and then comment on keeping your best sales representatives.

Where do I find potential top sales performers?
The traditional way to recruit star salespeople is to take them from your competitors. They come with a portfolio of industry knowledge, customer relationships, and market savvy, and they require very little training. Two quick points—it pays to know your competitor's best salespeople and if you decide to recruit your competitor's employees, you can assume they will respond in kind.

If you don't personally know whom to target, you can contract with a recruitment specialist to identify candidates and solicit their interest. The approach can be expensive and is not a guarantee of producing one star after the next; however, it is time-tested and generally effective. Using recruiters also makes the act of directly contacting a competitor's sales staff less controversial.

Sometimes top performers will seek you out. If your business is a 'hot' brand or generating 'buzz' in your markets, the phone will start to ring! Success attracts success...salespeople are often attuned to getting in on momentum plays and working for top companies.

Hundreds of thousands of sales managers find that their reality is a little different. Using the services of expensive recruiters and finding anxious stars waiting in the lobby are not realistic sources of talent. These managers constantly search for proven top performers but spend the vast majority of their efforts interviewing the mediocre and inexperienced—looking for a potential contributor with the ability to produce results now and become a star tomorrow.

Their best referrals are from current employees, business associates, friends, family, alumni associations and community organizations. They place internet job postings and local newspaper advertisements. Local or regional career and job fairs round out their recruitment channels. Businesses frequently provide non-sales employees an opportunity to learn to sell and move up.

Those who succeed as sales managers are always in a recruitment mode. Waiting for applicants to come to them is not an option. They develop the ability to recognize and recruit talent. Most will confess to learning from mistakes, creating a recruitment network and becoming students of the personal qualities required by their business model and markets.

 I always kept a few business cards in my pocket to give to potential recruits. Any and every business and personal activity was fair game for discovering an opportunity. I have hired sales candidates I met at restaurants, in airports, on vacations, while shopping or attending weekend soccer games with my children. Necessity is truly the mother of inventiveness!

Professional sales managers understand that once you find top performers and those on the way to achieving this status, it pays to work tirelessly to keep them! The easiest way to reduce your dependence on recruitment is to select carefully, then train, grow and retain the valuable salesmen and women who work in your organization.

Qualifying top performers and future sales professionals

What I discovered from years of recruiting and managing salesmen and women is that what they have already accomplished in a career or put on a resume is not as important as the personal qualities they possess.

Experience is certainly valuable! The recruitment challenge is in judging the validity of the past and applying it to your specific needs. In *Smart Selling! Your Roadmap To Becoming a Top Performer*, Chapter 1 reveals the four types of salespeople and the assignments most appropriate for each profile. It's worth your time to review the material.

You will need to decide what type of salesperson best fits the assignment you have available. Past selling success does not necessarily translate to a new assignment. A quick example: A successful sales executive who comes from a highly scripted selling environment with a well-defined support system may struggle to work in a very unstructured entrepreneurial environment. Similarly, entrepreneurial salespeople may feel uncomfortable with a very predictable and constrained environment.

Selling into a new industry or having to learn complex new product specifications can prove to be difficult, even if the candidate is initially willing to try! In reality, top pharmaceutical sales representatives may not be able to transition into becoming top-performing marine turbine salesmen. I have seen too many of these well-intentioned experiments fail. The bottom line on experience is...despite its value, it is not always a reliable indicator of future performance...and it is the future performance which really matters to you!

1	High Energy
2	Focus
3	Fearless
4	Urgency and Persistence
5	Positive Attitudes
6	Communicators
7	Knowledgeable
8	Efficient
9	Leaders
10	Balance

So what should recruiters of sales talent look for? Start by exploring the ten personal skills which are second nature to top performers. These skills make candidates with or without significant sales maturity and experience worthy of serious consideration. The best hires have refined these skills and are willing to discuss why they are important to their present and future plans for success in sales.

A candidate who has high energy is interesting, one who admits to being less energetic raises a caution flag. Someone who struggles to communicate is at a disadvantage. A recruit who is focused on being in sales and achieving real success has my attention! Positive attitudes are always desirable. If the applicant is nervous or uncomfortable in your presence, ask yourself: How will they present themselves and the business to prospects? The next step is to ask two questions: Would I buy from this person? Would my prospects and customers buy from this person?

If you can positively answer those questions, you are ready to explore why the candidate wants to work for you and your business. The answers are certain to surprise. I have heard everything from:

> This is a great place to learn!
> The company is a winner.
> I understand you offer the best commission plan.
> I just want a job.
> I saw your sign on the building.
> I really don't know why I should work here, but I
> have to work somewhere!

Look for a statement which reflects focus and reveals a plan. "This opportunity fits my current career path, and it is also an important step in my plan to..."

Robert was still enjoying his good fortune. Not being called to the now infamous forecast meeting was a true gift from heaven! Instead he was assigned to hire three salespeople ASAP.

He created a careful plan. One hire would be done by a recruiter, the candidate would be the best seasoned salesperson available from one of Baker's smaller competitors. The word was out that AG International employees were off limits. The second hire was to be less experienced and come from the various job postings HR had placed on the web—with a minimum of three years B-2-B sales experience. The final recruit was anticipated to be from the employee referral plan with the same experience level. The bonus offer was currently $2,500; so there was no shortage of people being recommended. A number of salespeople had given Robert resumes from personal friends and relatives.

"He called again...asking for you."

"Who?"

Robert's Administrative Assistant shook her head in disbelief,

"James Scott Cuddyer, I gave you the resume."

"Why does he keep calling me?"

"He wants an interview!"

"He has no sales experience."

"I know, but he's not going away until he at least talks with you. Could you please...please...call him and end this thing?"

Robert's call never happened.

The receptionist interrupted the discussion to introduce Robert's visitor. "Mr. Cuddyer is here to see you."

From his chair, Robert stared up at one of the largest humans he had ever encountered. Cuddyer wasted no time grabbing Robert's hand. His grip was like a vice. "Sorry, I have to learn to control my energy."

Standing at over 6'5", his 225 pounds of pure muscle was just plain intimidating. Asking him to leave was not an option.

"We both graduated from UT same year, can't say I recognize you. I was in the area and thought I would try my luck...the receptionist was really helpful."

"Sit down...please. Let me see if I can find your resume."

James Scott sat down. He filled the chair and more. His closely cropped hair and clean cut appearance made him look even larger. "I have a copy if you can't find one." Reaching into his jacket pocket he extracted the carefully folded document and presented it to Robert as if it was an original work of art.

"U.S. Marine Corps right after college...discharged last month. I'm looking for a sales position. I want to get with a top company, gain some experience and become a business executive. I understand you are looking for salespeople. I have done a lot of research about your company and competitors. This is a great business...rapid growth."

"We are...but, we're trying to find people with at least three years' experience. Your resume looks a little light on that count."

"Actually, I have worked at a number of sales positions both in high school and while putting myself through UT. Sold office equipment, automobiles, shoes, all types of stuff. I love sales, great way to make a living. I really enjoy working with people...helping people. I'm a Business major, going to get an MBA at night school, I start officially next semester."

"Sales is hard work, especially when you're just learning."

Cuddyer smiled and leaned forward as if to share a secret. His voice had a tested leadership quality. "Being a Marine Officer is hard work, keeping a platoon of leathernecks alive is not for the faint-hearted. I understand hard work, sacrifice and responsibility. I intend to be a very good sales executive and I am prepared to be held accountable for delivering results."

Reeling...Robert fell back to his next question. "How did you learn

139

about Baker Industries?"

"I read this story about Mr. Bob Kelly and how he started the business out of the trunk of his car, built it into a big company, turned it over to his kid brother and then went back to carrying a sales bag. Said he just enjoyed the opportunity to sell. That's my kind of marine!"

Robert was still tongue-tied. He glanced up to see Bob looming larger than life in his doorway.

"Actually, I failed at three businesses before this got off the ground...dumb luck. A friend gave me a printing press to sell for him and away it went. My brother did the heavy lifting."

The young marine practically jumped to attention.

Kelly introduced himself, "Career in sales?"

"Yes, sir...at least for five years. I hope to build a business just like this when I get further down the road."

"Family?"

"Yes, sir...three young children and two older brothers both in sales."

"Sales doesn't come with any guarantees."

"Understood, but I'm confident if I work hard and smart, learn the trade, I expect you would treat me fairly. Any chance I could work with you?"

Kelly laughed heartily, "Once you get to know me, you may sincerely regret asking for that assignment! Robert will take good care of you...Tell me about your research..."

Cuddyer walked through market information and statistics. He displayed a grasp of Baker's product line and the competitors. His energy and enthusiasm were contagious, crisp and efficient.

"Pretty nice presentation. Most of your facts are right on. Our edge has always been in sales. We are just better salespeople than AG. They rely on engineering more then we do. Impressive work...So, how are you going to explain the missing sales experience?"

"I can't, but what I can do is to convince you of my interest in this position, my willingness to learn and the fact that I am focused on succeeding. I can't afford to give up any more time. I'm already a few years older than most new..."

Kelly raised his hands in surrender.

James Scott Cuddyer extended his hand to Kelly. "Does that mean I have your vote of confidence I'll become a top salesman for Baker Industries if I get the chance?"

"Well, James, let me just make one comment for what it's worth. I would sure buy a Baker Press from you!"

Kelly's stare made it clear what he wanted Robert to do.

"You know, Bob, I think Karen should meet James...second opinion?" Without a moment's hesitation—Kelly grabbed the new recruit by the shoulder and led him off to Karen's office.

Cuddyer was a smart man. He quickly sized Karen up. "I expect you are the decision maker."

The chess match had began.

"If I was the decision maker, tell me what I would see as your strengths and what should I worry about?"

"Mature, focused, good communicator, hard worker, energetic and a leader."

"And?"

"I would want to be sure I could quickly transition into sales, deliver some deals, and make the customers feel comfortable, not intimidated."

"Could you do that?"

"Yes. I believe I can."

"What would you need from me?"

"A mentor—someone to show me the ropes. It will make the transition go much quicker."

"Work for Robert?" Karen had hammered the open issue in James Scott Cuddyer's mind.

"I assume this is 'fish or cut bait' time?"

Karen sat expressionless, staring at Cuddyer.

"I will do that, Karen, and..."

"Before we consider a second interview, I would like to have you meet some our senior sales executives. Are you available for a quick lunch tomorrow?"

"I am. Perhaps we could finish getting acquainted and, of course, review an offer?"

Karen asked Cuddyer to give her and Bob a second...

"Pretty tough on him."

"Did I come across as difficult? Sorry! Could you introduce him to Don Brown, and have him see how good Mr. Cuddyer's sales skills are? If he checks out, I will be on my best and most charming at lunch."

"Karen, we...you...need a very good salesman and, in time, a sales manager."

She sensed a very slight transformation in Bob's demeanor...her instincts told her change was afoot!

How to professionally recruit

Hiring top performers requires both parties ultimately to agree to work together. In some markets, economies, and moments in time, employers have the upper hand; in other circumstances, potential employees are in control. Offering a candidate a position they decline because the recruitment process was poorly handled is a lost opportunity. Losing an applicant to a competitor who out-recruited you is just as annoying!

The interview process is a window. You examine the qualifications of a candidate and they look at you and your business. Each party has the option to walk away if they are unimpressed, uncomfortable or dissatisfied. As a sales manager, you want to limit the reasons a qualified candidate has to select someone else as their next employer.

Professional sales recruiters have learned to qualify candidates, even when it requires asking difficult questions, all the while communicating a genuine sense of appreciation for the candidate's interest and participation. They know that at the moment in time when it's decided the candidate is the person you want on your team, the applicant must be in a positive frame of mind and anxious to receive and accept your offer.

Rules to recruit by:
- Don't mislead anyone about your intentions for the interview. If the selection process is just starting, say so! If you are on a fast track to a final decision, say so!
- Be on time and prepared. Review resumes before the candidate arrives.
- Polite, helpful and welcoming! Candidates are always treated as important and respected guests.
- Candidates deserve your full attention during your time together.
- Discuss qualifications and ask questions. Never interrogate a candidate or criticize a response!
- Be candid about the issues you want to explore or have clarified.
- Answer the candidates questions to the best of your ability.
- Reveal the timetable for filling the position and the intermediate decision steps.
- Respect the fact candidates may not be able to answer questions which encroach on either competitive information or proprietary material.
- Follow-up on the commitments you make for scheduling second interviews, conversations or final decisions. No one wants to be left in the dark!

The salespeople you most want to be part of your team are inevitably those who are in the greatest demand. They know how to sell, qualify and make judgments about people. They want to work for managers who can advance their careers and successful businesses. Hiring them is about serving mutual interests—theirs and yours! Recruiting mistakes will cost you dearly with this audience.

Marginal candidates will tolerate recruitment gaffs. Why? They have limited options. If you find yourself beset with marginal hires, the approach you use to recruit is one of the first issues you should examine.

Candidates who will agree to anything, question little and accept whatever you offer are the ones you should be most cautious about. If they are new to the profession or generally inexperienced, their zeal to get a career started is understandable and smart. Experienced sales people who exhibit these characteristics are either looking for a temporary home or burdened with other issues. Just proceed carefully and keep probing.

References are an ongoing and difficult test for managers recruiting salespeople. Very few candidates will present anything other than glowing references. Past employers and sales peers fearing a variety of real and potential legal liabilities are highly unlikely to offer you much official assistance. Background checks may or may not be reliable or possible.

The best approach is to recruit candidates you know personally or who have been vouched for by people whose judgment you trust. Unfortunately, for many sales managers that potential pool of candidates is far too small. You can limit your exposure by checking references directly with the candidates' past managers, rather than relying on Human Resource administrators.

Ask direct questions about the claims you have received. "Did she achieve 200% of plan last year?" Stay away from subjective questions such as, "Was he a good person? Was she well-liked?" Subjective questions will get you subjective answers from people with 'who knows what' agenda!

Some employers will bend over backwards to help an ex-employee or soon to be ex-employee find a new position because of guilt or because they want their current problem to become...your problem. Listen carefully to what ex-managers say or refuse to say. Unfortunately, candor and truthful responses have given way to non-committal babble.

If you are getting mixed signals from your reference calls, you may want to pause and ask the candidate for either clarification or to provide another set of names to call. References have become a good example of the maxim—Buyer Beware!

Experienced sales managers can recount, all excuses aside, about mistakes they have made. These recruitment miscues come with the responsibility for hiring salespeople. I have made them and you will too.

Effective sales recruiting requires you to judge the value of your candidate's past experience. Explore the sales and personal performance skills they possess now and project to grow towards. Decide if they have a career plan which aligns with your open position. Finally, ask a simple question—Would you buy from this person?

▶ Don Brown was very impressed with James Scott Cuddyer. "He has great sales instincts, more experience than the resume indicates and, most important, is really focused on a sales career. I called a mutual friend who works with one of his brothers, she said his brother is a super successful manufacture's representative."

Cuddyer was smart and a tough negotiator.

Karen was at her personable and witty best, just as promised. Kelly and Brown were along for support and, of course, lunch. They listened with interest as she extolled the virtues of Baker Industries and closed in for a commitment.

Cuddyer just took it all in, "Karen, I guess you and I got off on the wrong foot yesterday."

"Well, let's just say you caught me on a rare bad day!"

"No, actually I wanted to apologize to you. I really blew the question you asked me...my fault...inexcusable."

Kelly was about to speak, then hesitated, "What question was that James?"

"The one about working for Robert."

"Oh."

"I thought about my answer...kept me awake half the night. I just can't do that, Ma'am."

Kelly choked on his sandwich.

Brown groaned.

Karen went blank.

"Do you mean you're having...?"

"No, no second thoughts. I just can't...won't...work for Robert." Cuddyer, ever a marine, then sat in perfect silence and proceeded to attack his lunch.

"You have a problem with Robert?"

"Me? No, sir! You have a problem with him."

Kelly stiffened.

"I mean, I'm asking myself, 'Where is Robert?' Why is my new boss not sitting here? If he's not here now, what does that say about his ability to help me become a great salesperson?"

Karen giggled, then waved her finger at Cuddyer! "I guess I know you are a salesperson! Very well done."

His smile was pleasant, but it had an tiny edge of intensity.

She resumed, "I want to hire you. Now, we are going to find out if you take risks or if you are into security."

He never blanched.

"I, as you may know, have never been in the military; but I bet as a marine you were asked to do missions...some without any details...you did them because you trusted the people you worked for? Right?"

"Yes..."

"I want you to be part of this team. We will train you, test you and, in time, promote you...if you deliver results! You, for your part, will have to make a leap of faith on this issue and maybe a couple of others."

"I see."

She extended her hand and asked, "So James, do we have a deal or should I ask the infamous Mr. Kelly to plead my case?"

Training Salespeople

It costs real time and money to train a sales team. It costs even more to ignore this basic business investment! Training for a sales team falls into three broad categories: market education, product expertise and selling skills.

Training is important to all businesses, well-heeled or not! The scope of budgets may be dramatically different but the need is constant. Turnover, inexperience and a surge in hiring all conspire to create the need for educational programs. The alternative is the inefficient and costly 'teach yourself' approach. The availability of a well-run and structured program is a powerful recruiting tool.

Becoming an expert about the markets, industries and businesses to which you sell increases your ability to deliver valuable information and knowledge to prospects and customers. It is a skill top performers understand and all salespeople should aspire to achieve. Business savvy gives you an edge in creating credibility and winning competitive contests. The rapidity of changes occurring in your market should dictate the frequency of this training.

Product expertise is no less important...it's difficult to sell the value of products you don't thoroughly understand. Prospects are uncomfortable doing business with salespeople who are ill-informed about the benefits, features and functions of their products. I suspect you would feel the same way!

Sales skill training is a must for new salespeople and the experienced members of your team. When you build and work closely with a sales team, you learn which skills are generally well developed and which are lacking. If you have the foresight to adopt a customer-focused business sales methodology, this is an excellent opportunity to familiarize the sales-force with its application. Every sales practitioner regardless of their experience level can benefit from training. For some the material may be completely new, for others it will serve as a refresher. On-going professional education keeps a team fresh and focused! In my experience, training can really help a team bond and open communication channels.

Create an annual educational plan which lays out a concrete training schedule for the complete team. Individual plans may be needed for those salespeople who have a problem with specific sales or personal skills. Sometimes they may ask for this additional training, on other occasions you may prescribe tutoring. The assistance may include seminars, books, self-improvement courses or general educational offerings.

Training can be accomplished without infringing on your team's prime selling time which is often the major excuse offered by those who want to avoid this subject. Try scheduling training events during lunch hour, evenings, weekends, or as part of a sales meeting. It really just requires a bit of creativity! Training sessions should be engaging, entertaining and informative. They don't have to be boring and laborious!

One final observation, if you communicate and demonstrate a serious personal commitment to training...the salesforce will follow your lead.

Terminating Salespeople
Warning: I am not qualified to provide any legal advice in our discussion of this topic, nor is it my intention.

Sales managers are responsible for making decisions which often lead to the termination of salesmen and women. It is a sobering and difficult part of the responsibility entrusted to your care. Taking away a person's employment is a serious action. It's also governed by a significant body of employment laws and regulations at the Federal and State levels. Most businesses have crafted well-defined termination procedures to protect

146

their organization and managers. I do recommend that you consult with an attorney who has expertise in the field of employment law before you entertain any termination actions.

In general, terminations should occur when performance objectives are not met or when the rules of business conduct are breached. Managers who set clear and measurable performance standards and diligently communicate the rules of conduct serve their teams well. Why? They remove ambiguity from the grounds for termination decisions and discussions. The most contentious and difficult terminations occur when a surprised employee is held accountable for debatable or poorly communicated criteria resulting in the termination of their employment.

When salespeople understand the consequences for performance failure, they terminate themselves if they fail to achieve their goals.

Bob Kelly was the last to arrive in Daniel Kelly's office. He found a comfortable chair and sat without saying a word. Daniel was well into an animated conversation with his Vice President of Human Resources and Baker Industries legal team. A portable oxygen bottle sat at his side.

"I have made up my mind to terminate Al, his performance has been really disappointing. The scaled-back plan I agreed to has not been met! But, the worst part is he has really set us back with his recruiting failures. Robert was a premature promotion, Norton is a bad hire...terrible mistake. We are still short on salespeople. This is not the same VP of Sales I have relied on for the last 10 years! I think he has already left..."

The chief legal counsel cleared his throat, "Dan, he is going to leave in three short months. Why create a problem when we don't have to? Just let the three months expire and Al goes away quietly...please!"

"Why is this so complicated?"

"It's complicated because he's a long-term employee and you have done nothing to warn him of your dissatisfaction. Nothing, not a conversation or document to place him on any kind of notice."

"Are you saying I can't fire him?'

"No, Dan...you can do whatever you please. My job is to be certain you don't regret your decision...either personally or as the CEO."

Baker's lawyer paused and walked to the window...he stared at Dan, "As a friend, I am telling you, you are a physical wreck. You belong in a hospital which we both know is what your doctors have ordered. Al Winters has served the company well. He should be allowed to retire and whatever mistakes he has made...will get fixed."

147

Dan turned to his Vice President of HR, "Sally, what about Norton?"

"He's a different story. His employment agreement includes a one-year probationary period. We can terminate his employment without cause and..."

"And...what?"

"Al has extensive documentation in Norton's file including performance warnings and statements of failures. He has done an outstanding job of following our termination procedures step-by-step."

"I see, you are also opposed to Al's termination?"

"I surely am! But, I think he could be approached about leaving early...an early release to start his retirement. At the risk of being out of line, do you know Al's wife is terminal?"

Daniel sat as if frozen in time.

Bob broke the silence, "I'm going to need some time with Daniel."

"No one told me. I would certainly have remembered being told."

"For what it's worth, I didn't know either. However, it does explain Al's being so distracted."

"Bob...I?"

"Danny, you didn't want this job when I talked you into it. You have done more than I could have ever accomplished. Now we need to concentrate our efforts on getting you out of here and into a hospital!"

Bob Kelly, the founder and largest shareholder of Baker Industries, was about to take control of his business once again.

Al Winters flanked by Legal and HR met with Norton. "I am sorry, Norton. I need to tell you that we are going to terminate your employment. The reason for our action is your inability to reach the performance objectives—specifically, your team's sales quota which we mutually agreed upon. I formally notified you 30 days ago, and you acknowledged in writing that failure to achieve this month's plan would result in this action."

"I see...so it's come to this?"

"I am truly sorry your time at Baker has not worked out. We have a separation package for you, agreed to at the time of your hiring. I know how difficult this is for you."

"No, Al, it is difficult, but I made a mistake coming over here. I could have succeeded with more time and better support, but that's not gonna happen is it?"

"Norton, I believe we gave you ample opportunity to succeed. I can't give you any extensions."

Al got up and extended his hand to Norton. "I wish you the best of luck. Sally will take you through all the separation details and will be your contact for any assistance you need." He hesitated for a moment, then left the room.

Managing Resignations

There are two types of resignations—those you want to accept and those you wish to have withdrawn.

Every sales manager will work with salespeople who are difficult. They may have personality quirks which present challenges, struggle with countless other sales skills, argue with customers and annoy prospects. Yet they achieve plan! You coach them, motivate, train and re-train and still the issues remain. Frustrating! High-maintenance! When they decide to resign for a variety of reasons...you breathe a sigh of relief.

The best approach to those resignations you are comfortable accepting is to be polite, gracious and accommodating. I have sat and listened to many resignations that included rebukes, criticism of the company, its management and me personally. The information can be valuable, interesting, partially true or just nonsense. Learn from the comments, ignore the inappropriate stuff and wish them the best.

Resignations you wish to have withdrawn present a different challenge. Sometimes the underlying reason may be completely personal and beyond your control. It's impossible to tell a working spouse they should refuse to relocate with their partner. Family or health issues often dictate difficult decisions. The best you can do is to leave the door open for future re-employment or get very creative.

I have allowed salespeople to work from remote locations or from home offices rather than lose their services. Leaves-of-absence can be helpful for resolving personal issues. Accommodations can be permanent adjustments or just temporary changes. Just be careful you are not creating policies which can inadvertently change the face of your sales organization. Going the extra mile to keep your best performers is smart business and sends a responsible message to the rest of your salesforce.

What about resignations caused by the opportunity for promotion or better compensation arrangements? The stakes are always high when a top performer announces he or she is leaving for more money, a new title or more responsibility. Some sales managers will refuse to negotiate these issues, other managers believe that the best policy is to negotiate! Who is correct? Unfortunately, there is no one simple answer.

If you negotiate, the line may literally start to form at your door. The message becomes sales management can be coerced by resignations. The problem becomes worse if executive management injects itself into the fray. Refusing to negotiate may result in the loss of top performers and your sales team's achievement of plan. The correct approach is to step back from the brink and ask several questions.

Is this an employee who is acting reasonably and responsibly?
I have known salespeople to resign because they had been recruited for management assignments. The first question I always asked was, "Why do you want to be a manager?" The answers were sometimes surprising and occasionally troubling.

"I can't stand sales!" or "I want out from the quota plan!" doesn't speak well for a new manager.

"It's my next career step...and my long-term goal" sends a different message.

Salespeople leaving for more lucrative commission plans or greater base salaries should be able to explain why they believe they benefit by resigning. Is the increase a commitment or a promise contingent on something else?

I had a top performer resign to go to a competitor for substantially more money—a business that was unfortunately known for making and breaking promises to any and everyone. During our conversation, my salesperson revealed the quota he had to achieve to reach his new compensation figure. The number was so large...it defied imagination!

Doing some quick math, I demonstrated he could make even more by staying right where he was and delivering the same sales number. I also asked him if anyone at his new company had ever reached the sales goal he was given? "No," he revealed after withdrawing his resignation.

His emotions got the best of his judgment.

The point is, you need to probe and then understand the motivation behind the resignation. Has it been well-thought out or is it an emotional response? It's possible to reverse emotional decisions.

Does the ability to meet the request exist?
"I can't offer you what I don't have." It's not always possible to offer a counter-proposal. Perhaps your business doesn't have the ability or desire to pay base salaries above $150K. You may not have a sales office in California or have an immediate sales management assignment to offer. The concession being requested may not exist; and as a result, you have little choice but to accept the resignation. If you can meet the demand, you will have to answer the next question.

150

Are they likely to succeed in the position for which they are asking?
We are not all capable of doing what we desire. The accomplishment of securing a job does not equate to success in performing the assignment! Your evaluation of talent may be different than that of another employer who may be willing to take risks that you will not accept. You may have knowledge about your employees others don't!

Top sales performers do not always make great sales managers. Being successful as a sales support representative does not mean you are ready for a sales assignment. Not all sales managers are destined to be Vice Presidents of Sales. You will have to decide for yourself if the person in question meets your business's criteria for the assignment they're seeking.

Am I willing to counter-offer?
A truly difficult decision! Why? Sales managers simply don't want to lose competent salespeople. Executives also don't want to send a signal that encourages resignations as a way of getting promotions, raises or other concessions. Counter-offers should be made when someone, deemed valuable to your team, receives a proposal you have already contemplated. "You are already on our list of candidates for promotion!" The timing of your offer may have been preempted by another employer, but your plan to promote was already well under way. Employees will react more positively to counter-offers they come to understand have already been vetted and in the works. Your proposal should be clear, detailed and a best and final counter.

When a resignation is both unexpected and surprising in its scope, you may have little choice beyond gracious acceptance. Decisions made in haste and under the duress of deadlines controlled by others can be dangerous. Poorly thought-out counter-offers are often rejected and then viewed as a display of weakness or panic on the part of management. Remember, when you make a counter-offer, it will be publicly discussed. Other sales representatives will learn the details you have proposed and compare their own situations. Your sales team will also be exposed to any bidding which takes place between employers. Any counter-offer you make will likely be brought to your adversary for a re-bid of their own. The path quickly becomes a very slippery slope!

This discussion should also serve as a reminder to pro-actively protect your team members by advancing their careers as quickly as possible. The salespeople you most want to keep will have options beyond your immediate business. You need to be creative and enterprising in protecting and retaining your top performers!

Is there a compromise solution available?

Sometimes employees will express interest in or suggest a compromise as they present a resignation. They offer a resignation but, in fact, what they want is change, a new opportunity or the promise of a brighter future. They will leave, but it's not their first choice.

> "I have been offered a management position which I know you can't offer, but I would consider working as an account executive for a year if you will consider me for a management assignment in the future."

Compromises that fit within your sales management plans and strategy should be carefully considered. Those which are beyond the boundaries you foresee are best rejected. What you owe your employees is candor and honesty. Don't make expedient promises you can't or will not keep. No one should be misled about their career opportunities.

> "I am willing to offer you an account executive position, but your chances of becoming a manager without a significant growth in your leadership skills is not very likely! Are you willing to work at developing these skills? Can you accept the fact you may not become a manager in this company in the foreseeable future?"

Compromises are only valuable if they are agreed to and honored by both parties.

The rumors of Daniel Kelly's failing health were swirling at Baker and throughout the industry. Salespeople were being asked by prospects and customers for information and guidance. The uncertainty was starting to impact the business and its sales team.

At 11 p.m. on Thursday evening, Karen's home fax machine spat out a single page document. She stared at the paper in disbelief. The Board of Directors had issued a short press statement.

> *Robert Kelly, founder of Baker Industries, has been elected Chairman and CEO. He succeeds Daniel Kelly who has resigned as a result of a serious health issue. Our thoughts and prayers are with Dan and his family.*

> *The Board is delighted to have Bob once again lead the company. His management and strength as an executive created and grew Baker to its present position. His vision for the future will guide the business to its next stage and beyond.*

Karen knew this would be a very difficult time to announce her resignation. Sleep would come hard this evening.

Bob Kelly was also awake for the night—too many decisions. Who to rely on...how to get the sales team on track and delivering its numbers?

He saw the light in her office when he arrived a little before 6 a.m. "Karen, you look worse than I feel! Sorry, I meant to say..."

"No offense taken, Bob. I can't imagine how bad I must look. I am so sorry about Dan, will he be okay?"

"I really can't say, it's just too soon to tell how it will all work out."

"Bob, I really need to talk with you, the sooner the better. I want to tell you about a offer I have debated for couple of weeks."

"No decisions until we talk. I reached a decision a couple of weeks ago which you have to hear, and then think about, before you say anything about whatever it is you're debating."

He disappeared as quick as he had appeared.

Al Winters was already waiting in Bob's office. Bob offered him a coffee. "Picked it up at Geno's this morning!"

"Bob, I want you to know I have really made a mess of this year. No excuses, just bad decisions."

"I would prefer for you to stay on, Al. We have worked together for a long time, I hired you when...10 years ago?"

"I have come to resign, Bob, because it's the right thing to do. The business is no longer my top priority and I think we both know that's an understatement. I took my eye off the ball and it showed!"
They both sipped on their coffees and sat silently.

"Are you sure Geno made this today?"

"Al, luckily no resignations are being processed this morning. I will grant your request to retire three months early in return for a consulting arrangement. Give the new VP of Sales a few hours a week of advice and maybe an occasional call to a customer. A smooth transition with a lot of reassurance for the customers. Write it up with Sally, stop by tomorrow morning and we can get it executed."

"Bob, tomorrow is Saturday."

"That's okay. I'll be here...try a different coffee place in case Geno's is closed!"

Al wished in some simple way he could turn the clock back and work with Bob again. One last mea culpa. "Hey, the new sales VP...she was here at 5 a.m. this morning. I really blew that one. Well, after picking up your sales faux pas, it's your turn to fix my recruitment disaster."

Kelly knew Winters would be back...just as he was. One more task before meeting Karen. A conference call to finish and a document to sign—both of which would change the future of Baker Industries forever.

He muttered to himself, "I started on a shoestring and made good decisions, but this one is literally betting it all." Rubbing his forehead, he executed the agreement.

The place reeked of garlic, old chairs and worn tablecloths. The crowd was too focused on Geno's food to pay much attention to either Bob or Karen.

"Wow. I know I looked bad this morning, but this place sure makes me feel like a very fashionable executive."

"I have a long history with this place...very discriminating about who I bring here!"

"I bet."

Geno waited the table personally and was quick to join the conversation, "Mr. Bob started his business right here! Closed all his big sales at my restaurant, this table! Without my food, he would be nothing. I told him...they buy because of the food!" The food started to arrive and Geno remarked. "Mr. Bob, I can tell this is a very, very important sale."

Karen flinched. Kelly seemed to be beaming with confidence, "Geno, let's hope I have one last sale in me—here in a place I regard as hallowed ground."

Kelly wasted little time, "You eat and I'll talk...okay? First, going back to AG will accomplish what they want but will not give you the opportunity you deserve. You left them to work in a business you described as a momentum player with rapid growth and fast-paced. Okay, we hit some bumps in the road, you more than accomplished your job, and now it's time to get back on track. Except this time, Karen, you get to drive the strategy."

Before she could respond he made one additional point, "If they want you back now, fine, make them wait another year or so and they'll make a better offer! They move at two speeds—slow and slower—which I believe are the exact words you used to describe their culture. Okay, not another word about AG ever!"

Karen stared at Bob.

"What?"

"Nothing, I'm listening to your presentation."

"So I asked myself, 'How do I convince her to become the VP of Sales?' I could try to buy your participation; but, I decided instead I should give you the ability to determine what it is you need to run this sales team and get the growth moving again and let you tell me...what you want me to do to help you become successful. That's exactly what I would have asked for if I was considering the job."

"What makes you sure I'm ready for this, especially under these circumstances?"

"Well, your resume is not the reason. It's really my judgment of your character and personal skills. I have come to believe you will get this job accomplished because success matters to you. I expect you will make mistakes, ask for help and learn. I worked for you, Karen! You won my respect and everybody else's on your team. We know what being a good...no, great VP of Sales is all about. Incidentally, I offered to retain Al Winters to mentor you and just to be a general sounding board. He said he would serve only if you approve of his participation!"

She hesitated and Kelly continued, "The truth is most of us are not ready for the assignments we are put in. I wasn't ready to start this business or to manage it, but I did and I learned along the way!

"Do you need an answer this moment?"

"No, but I do want to understand—why can't you make a commitment?"

"Bob, I would have to rescind my commitment to AG. As much as I respect your offer, there are also relationships on the other side to consider."

His resolve was rock solid and his eyes reflected a steel will. "Do you believe in what we are doing at Baker? Do you want to be personally accountable for driving our success?"

"I do."

"Sounds to me like you have made a decision."

"I have...I want the job!"

"I can end the AG problem." His cellphone buzzed loudly, he stared hard at it. "Sorry, I have to take this call." He listened and said only, "Thanks." He handed the phone to Karen. "Some news you should hear from your ex-employer."

Karen recognized Hans Merkels voice, the CEO of AG Industries, who told her they now worked for the same company and both reported to Mr. Robert Kelly.

He had never seen her blush.

"I guess I really did make the right decision!"

He smiled and said, "I never intended to let you make the wrong decision. So, now you know! Big job, Karen, and time is in short supply."

"Why acquire AG?"

"I felt we needed to move them out of the way eventually, our slow sales just accelerated my timetable."

"Bob, I got a call from Cuddyer this morning. He and his brother are in Japan."

"His brother...the manufacturer's rep?"

"Actually, I retained his services for the Far East market...commission only with a little cash up front...to get us started in Japan. He sold six presses for $15 million to Nippon United Publishing. We don't have a sales revenue problem...not this year!"

She had never seen him blush. "How big is this new job?" she asked.

"For now, you will run the new Baker sales organization in North America. We'll create one global team for which you will have full responsibility, as soon as you're ready! Sally will take you through our formal offer tomorrow and then present any changes you request, which I will approve without objection. I will do that because I know you will be fair and that you realize your true rewards will come from delivering measurable results."

"Okay...excellent."

"How about we spend our time discussing what you want to do with your sales organization, and some strategy ideas I want you to consider for the remainder of this year? Then you have to tell me all about this sale in Japan!"

Bob winked at the ever-hovering Geno, who was quite enjoying the sale. His mind kept repeating the sage advice he received years ago:

"Hire good people...smart people, give them real responsibility, motivate them, support them, hold them accountable and good things will happen!"

TEST YOUR KNOWLEDGE

1. The success of a sales manager is directly tied to the ability to recruit, train and terminate salespeople and manage resignations.
   True/False

2. Recruiting salespeople is:
   ❏ Generally pretty easy to accomplish.
   ❏ A real commitment of both time and effort.
   ❏ Not something good managers do very often.
   ❏ An impossible task to do very well!

3. Experience is the most important indication of future success.
   True/False

4. Two important questions to ask yourself about any sales candidate:
   ❏ Do they look like a successful sales executive?
   ❏ Did they make plan in their last job?
   ❏ Would I buy from this person?
   ❏ Would my prospects buy from this person?

5. Professional recruiters make sure candidates understand they are lucky to be given an interview.
   True/False

6. Rules to recruit by include:
   ❏ Be on time and be prepared.
   ❏ Don't fully disclose your selection process.
   ❏ Be candid about the issues you want to explore and clarify.
   ❏ If a candidate offers an opinion you disagree with, let them know they're wrong!

7. It costs real time and money to train a salesforce.
   True/False

8. Terminations of salespeople should occur when performance objectives are not met or when _____

   _____

9. Resignations should be accepted without hesitation. When a salesperson resigns, they have breached a bond of trust.
   True/False

Sales Compensation Plans

Much like a flashing neon sign in the dark of night, sales compensation plans will grab the attention of your sales team. Why? The plan details the terms and conditions of a salesperson's required performance:

- How much sales revenue must a salesperson produce?
- How will salespeople be compensated for producing revenue?
- Which customers, prospects, geography, and/or products are they responsible to sell?
- When are the sales to be closed?
- How will a sale be judged as complete and accepted?
- What rules govern commission payments?
- What makes the plan official?

Quite simply, this is your written contract with each member of the sales team! How sales people earn commissions is very, very important—to them and to their employers. Effective sales managers leverage the focus a compensation plan provides, they make certain their goals, leadership and communications are perfectly aligned with the rewards the compensation plan prescribes. Salespeople will learn, dissect and memorize the details of their compensation plan. They will then proceed to maximize the financial rewards the plan offers! Which is good, right?

The answer is all about organizational alignment. If the plan is well-thought out and carefully constructed to meet your business goals, the answer is Yes! But, if you have a poorly constructed plan which rewards salespeople for doing things you really do not want to stress, you have a major challenge!

Let me give you an all-too-real example:

A new sales plan is introduced which heavily rewards selling an existing product line by offering extraordinary commissions and bonus payments. The same plan provides for very modest commissions on the company's brand new product line.

The executive management team, in its excitement about introducing a long overdue new product, assumed the sales team would quickly abandon the older product offerings in favor of the new easier-to-sell product line, regardless of a much lower commission rate.

"We didn't want sales to just completely abandon the old, we just assumed they would really work the new line..."

The sales staff may have embraced the new product if not for those extraordinarily generous commissions. It literally paid for the sales team to ignore the new and continue working the old! The sales compensation plan was out of alignment with management's real business strategy! We're going to examine each of the crucial components in a sales compensation plan and offer you some guidance.

How much sales revenue must a salesperson produce?

This is often referred to as a sales quota. This personal accomplishment is required to maintain one's good standing within the sales team and the business. Sales quotas are a reflection of the revenue budgeting process we reviewed earlier, as well as a mix of historical performance criteria, marketplace guidelines and strategic business decisions. Jobs in sales and across the entire business are tied to achieving quota!

Different sales assignments or sales positions will carry different quotas. Senior account executives have different responsibilities from a junior sales associate and will carry more quota. New recruits may be given start-up quotas during transition periods. As a general rule, every salesperson with an equivalent job description should also have the same quota assignment.

Most businesses and sales managers over-assign quota. If a company determines it must have $10MM of sales to meet its planned performance, it will often pass out $11MM in quota. Why? Since not every salesperson on the team will succeed in reaching plan, the cushion provides coverage for performance shortfalls.

Over-assignment also partially protects managers from the effects of resignations and terminations. Losing 20% or more of your sales team annually will give you a quick dose of managerial reality. How can I manage to quota when I'm short-staffed and breaking in new hires? The answer is planning, working to retain your salespeople, constant recruitment and a cushion referred to as over-assignment.

How will salespeople be compensated for producing revenue?

The total compensation plan for sales practitioners typically encompasses three forms of payment: base salary, commissions and bonus payments. Base salary is the guaranteed cash flow you are providing during a salesperson's employment. They may or may not earn commissions or bonus payments but their paycheck will reflect the agreed upon base salary.

What percentage of the compensation plan should be paid as base? The answer is a function of the risk and reward formula you decide to extend. Do you want to require the sales staff to sell in order to pay their bills or will your approach be less demanding? Some sales plans offer very low base salaries and focus instead on earned commission payments. These plans are referred to as being highly leveraged. Other plans reflect just the opposite approach—high base salaries, modest commissions. Some salespeople will look for highly leveraged plans, others will avoid working under high-risk compensation arrangements! They focus instead on positions offering higher base salaries. Occasionally, a business will create sales compensation plans which are built on base salary and bonuses. They remove commissions from the plan entirely.

I have worked as a commission-only salesperson and with plans in which commissions were only 35% of the total compensation package. I never felt sales plans heavily weighted to base salary were intrinsically more secure or desirable. In my experience, plans weighted to base salary are rarely as lucrative as the highly leveraged. Just remember, all salespeople are ultimately held accountable for results. You either deliver results or you move on, regardless of high-base salaries or commissions-only compensation arrangements.

A business which has a limited cash flow or working capital resources often wants to extend heavily weighted commission plans. Salespeople are paid from the cash they generate!

Companies also learn to balance their sales compensation plans with a recruitment strategy. Your industry or market may dictate that you offer a certain type of compensation plan to get the quality sales representatives you need.

The other business reality of this equation—a sales organization that offers commissions as its core compensation arrangement—will experience significant turnover if its salespeople are not making money regardless of who is at fault. Leverage often cuts in both directions!

Bonus payments may be made for achieving a quota, acquiring new accounts, securing references, selling specific products, accuracy in forecasting, limiting discounts, collecting payments with orders or countless other desirable actions. They reflect extraordinary accomplishments which are valuable to the sales team and the business.

Whatever leverage you infuse into your compensation plan, be certain it is equitably applied. Standardized job descriptions and sales assignments should reflect equalized compensation plans. Sales teams in which people perform the same basic job, but have different compensation plans, are ripe for discord! Compensation plans need to reflect your philosophy for paying sales representatives and not be a testimony to negotiation skills or recruitment compromises.

162

Which customers, prospects, geography, and/or products are they responsible to sell?

The territorial part of the assignment! The dictionary defines territory as, *an area in which one has certain rights or for which one has responsibility with regard to a particular type of activity.* Well-run sales teams have clearly defined territories—each team member knows to whom they sell and what product or service they may offer. The territory they are assigned becomes the focus of their sales efforts.

Territory is not always geographic. It can just as easily be an assigned list of names, a call list, every third person through the door, or those who ask about a specific product. Whatever method you use to determine the assigned responsibility, it should be equitable. Each salesperson should have the same opportunity to succeed! The opportunity may be 30 accounts or 3000 names on a list, just be certain the playing field is level!

The worst performing sales teams are often riddled with inequitable territories and "special" compensation plans for select individuals.

> *I still marvel at a particularly bad sales team that I had inherited. It featured one person assigned to every account West of the Mississippi River, and 40 representatives to the East. They managed 30 accounts each while "Mr. West" controlled hundreds. He had the exact same quota as his colleagues. And, not surprisingly, he beat plan and earned outrageous commissions each year while everyone else starved for opportunities! His "special" deal damaged the rest of the team and the business until it was fixed.*

Even clearly defined territories are the subject of disputes. A salesperson finds an account in a colleague's territory and begins to work the opportunity. The account may be a subsidiary or affiliate of one in their book of business. The reason for working in someone else's territory will always have some underlying reasoning attached. Sales managers have to constantly maintain order and territorial integrity.

I always used two simple rules to resolve disputes. First, the person doing the sales work gets credit for their efforts. Second, working outside your assigned territory without prior disclosure and management approval is grounds for being stripped of the order you worked to achieve! My sales teams understood both rules and the consequences of breaking them!

When are the sales to be closed?

The sales compensation plan should clearly spell out when quota must be achieved. Is quota to be reached monthly, quarterly or perhaps annually?

163

Many businesses assign an annual quota plan but prescribe how it is to be reached on a monthly or quarterly basis.

Why? Very few companies can financially afford to wait until year's end to book orders and discover how the salesforce is performing. The smarter approach is to ask the sales team to deliver a steady stream of orders and cash flow!

Compensation plans often provide for accelerated commission rates for exceeding monthly, quarterly or annual quotas. A monthly target of $100,000 may be commissioned as follows: 6% for the first $50,000, 8% for $50,001 to $100,000. All sales revenue in excess of monthly quota is commissioned at 10%! The same concept can be applied to quarterly and annual targets.

How will a sale be judged as complete and accepted?
Must accounts be shipped, invoiced and paid before a sale is recognized? What about merchandise return policies? Are commissions reversed if a customer fails to pay an invoice? Every business will have its own rules governing the final recognition of a sale. Compensation plans should disclose those same criteria, so sales representatives know when a transaction has reached final disposition.

I worked for a company that changed its policy of paying commission from an 'on order basis' to a 'final payment' method. The change was made by a financial officer with no notification or explanation. The sales team literally revolted! The CEO was forced to personally rescind the policy before the damage became significant. The episode left a large portion of the sales team with a diminished level of trust in the management team. The ensuing year was marked with high turnover and poor morale. Don't under-estimate the impact of adjusting compensation plans.

No salesperson likes to hear the word "chargeback" or be informed about a reversed commission! Surprises on commission statements are a source of needless conflict. Everyone deserves to know the rules and to be notified of accounts or transactions that are potential problems. It is amazing how many of these challenges can be quickly fixed with a little teamwork and advance warning!

What rules govern commission payments?
The two most typical questions are: When are commissions paid, month-end, the 15th of each month or quarterly? Must you be a current employee in good standing to receive commissions? The answer is not as important as the disclosure and communication! Many businesses with-

hold commission payments for a short period of time when a salesperson resigns. The intent is to clear any potential conflicts before a final payment is issued. The policy simply protects everybody from unnecessary disputes.

Sales compensation plans may also include topics such as the terms of employment, statements about the importance of ethical personal and business behavior, termination practices, dispute resolution procedures and rules governing the solicitation of customers. You will need to decide the scope of the entire document.

What makes the plan official?

The plan should be reviewed with each individual salesperson and then signed by both parties. It then becomes the governing document in an important business relationship! The more comprehensive it is, the more valuable it will prove in resolving inevitable questions.

Any modifications to the plan should be in writing and fully communicated. Salespeople will carefully examine any changes to their compensation. You will want to be prepared to explain the reason for the change and the impact you are attempting to achieve. Actions which affect either how or what salespeople are paid will always be subject to second guessing and should be approached with care and caution. Disrupting a salesperson or sales team in the middle of their assignment can have serious consequences. I received this advice and it served me well: "The announcement of good news is always welcome...be very careful with everything else!"

Karen's first week as Vice President of Sales was not quite the celebration she had anticipated! The challenge of merging two sales teams was first and foremost, and the issue of sales compensation was at the center of a brewing storm.

The AG team was aghast at the rapidity of the acquisition and felt betrayed. They pridefully viewed themselves as the industry leader. The act of submission to Baker Industries and Karen, an ex-employee and former colleague, was difficult. The worst part was the anticipated realignment of territories and a significant difference in compensation philosophy.

The Baker sales team wanted AG's people cleared out of any competitive accounts immediately if not sooner!

"Only ten salespeople in North America. We can use perhaps five or seven to fill our open positions, and evaluate using them to replace our worst performers."

165

Don Brown and Smitty, who was about to speak, were less enthused, "Robert, you are assuming the best performers will want to stay and that may not be the case. I'm not sure if they will accept our approach to leveraged commission plans. These guys are used to big base salaries and large territory assignments. We have 40 sales territories, they have 10, covering the same piece of geography."

Karen interrupted, "We can't afford to lose the complete AG sales team. It would set us back months and what kind of message would that send to AG customers? Don, now that you and Smitty are responsible for managing this new sales organization, you have to think this through!"

They both exhaled and seemed to mutter in unison, "Great! I think this is exactly why I avoided becoming a sales manager."

Robert, now responsible for sales administration and operations was not going to let this moment pass, "We have to resolve who stays, their territories and the compensation plans this week! Sorry, but it has to get done! The disruption will become a crisis if we don't."

Don turned to Robert, "Is it my imagination or have you gotten a lot smarter since you don't have to make any of these decisions?" They all laughed in frustration.

Karen knew most of the AG sales team. She also understood change would be difficult for many of them to accept. A transition plan was beginning to take shape in her mind.

"Robert, have Don and Smitty interview the three salespeople who are way behind plan. If they see something...okay. Otherwise, we'll give them termination packages."

"Done."

"The remaining seven stay. Four go into territories and the other three are put to work as partners who work with our sale representatives to transition the AG prospects and customers to our new company."

"Okay, but how are you going to deal with the compensation plan issue?"

"Our plan stays in place, no changes! The AG salespeople will be offered our plan, lower bases and higher commissions. I think we can use a draw, cash advances, to cover the difference in base salary for a transitional period of time. The territories are all equitable, small by their standards but..."

Robert was taking careful notes. "Let me run the draw stuff past HR and see if we can get buy-in to the concept. Sounds good...you're going to have to sell the idea to the new sales folks!"

Smitty was in Karen's office by 7 a.m. "I like the plan, as does Don, I will help you sell it if you want. Here's the list of the seven keepers, we really want the first two. They would be great additions."

Karen knew both Helen Black and Patti Scarzo well. They were both highly successful and, in fact, had out-performed Karen for several years—and neither missed an opportunity to remind her. They were the top performers at AG. The small conference room was full. Karen presented her proposal for merging the seven remaining AG International sales executives into the North American team. The mood was cordial and attentive.

Helen asked the first question, "Are you going to discuss sales comp?"

"I am. First, I have to tell you we have two very different approaches to this important issue."

"I like our plan much better than yours, Karen."

"I understand you do, but, in truth, our leveraged plan is just as rich as your current deal, we just get there differently."

"You get there with more risk and smaller territories!"

Karen knew Helen was going to push her and push hard, "Helen, you're a businesswoman, as well as a superb sales executive. I'm not going to play with this emotional issue. Our plan is more leveraged, we don't offer $100K base salaries, and our territories are smaller. I also have six salespeople who out-earned everyone in this room last year!"

"Oh, really?"

"I personally understand the change you are looking at, because I left AG to come over here. I gave up the plan you had for the one you are now considering. Baker is not going to change the sales approach that got it to this point and I would not recommend it do so!"

Helen sat quietly and Patti raised her voice, "Hey, Baker is the new owner of our business, we understand what that means. I for one believe I can compete with anyone as a sales executive. However, I would like to continue to pay my bills and this plan could present a problem."

Karen sensed Patti had personally handed her the opportunity she wanted, "No one—and I mean no one—wants you to be part of this team more than Bob Kelly and I do. I also do not want this transition to be difficult or painful. I want the decision to become part of the Baker sales team to be really simple and very lucrative!"

Robert distributed the new sales compensation plan and Karen went point by point through the document.

Helen's question was on tip of everyone's tongue. "So, the plan replaces the difference in base salary with draw which is non-recoverable for six months and then recoverable against commissions for another six months?"

"That's correct."

"This is a generous offer!"

"It is a sincere statement of our willingness to keep you focused on closing business and a gesture of how much we value your participation on this team."

"Thank you, Karen."

Patti and Helen and the five other sales representatives joined Karen, Robert, Don and Smitty for dinner at Geno's. Geno while serving dessert overheard Patti whisper, "Karen, you did good today, your generosity will pay real dividends in North America and it will be noticed overseas as well. Helen and I will both stay. We personally intend to help you lead this team. Why, by this time next year, I predict you will be Executive Vice President of Sales!"

Helen didn't let the opportunity pass, "Karen will be President and then CEO within five years!"

Karen's stunned expression was visible to Helen.

"Dear, they only make you VP of Sales to start the testing, the end game is to see if you are capable of running the business which you will be...with our help!"

Karen's cell phone flashed...Bob Kelly.

Geno congratulated his staff, "Miss Karen made another big sale this evening! Be sure you all treat her special...just like Mr. Kelly!"

Sales Compensation Plan

XYZ Company

Date:

Calendar Period of This Plan:

Sales Representative:

Sales Assignment/Territory:

Authorized Products/Service to be sold:

Quota Assigned: $000,000. per annum

    Prorated monthly and quarterly

Target Annual Income:

    Base Salary:

    Commissions at Plan:

    Bonus at Plan:

Commission and Bonus Plan:
- 2% on the amount of all sales up to your assigned quota.
- 3% on the amount of all sales after you have exceeded your annual plan.
- $1,000 p.a. bonus for timely submission of all required monthly forecasts. All forecasts are due the last business day of each month. Bonus is payable quarterly.
- $1,000 p.a. bonus for accurate forecasting. The achievement of 90% of your forecasted sales performance is required. The VP Sales may approve the payment of this bonus, if you exceed both your forecast and plan.

Sales Plan Terms and Conditions:
- Sales will be eligible for booking credit and commission payment when....
- How and when you get paid commission...
- Adherence to ethical business practices and policies....

Legal Obligations and Disclosures:
- How your employment status can affect commission payments...
- This plan is/is not a binding contractual agreement....
- Disputes are resolved by.....
- We reserve the right to make revisions to this plan....

Date Executed:_____

_____   _____
Company   Sales Representative

TEST YOUR KNOWLEDGE

1. Why are sales compensation plans important?

....

....

2. Compensation plans include:
   ❏ How much sales revenue must be produced.
   ❏ Which customers, prospects, geography or products must be sold.
   ❏ How compensation will be determined and paid.
   ❏ All of the above.

3. .... is the personal accomplishment required to maintain a good standing within the sales team and the business.

4. Total compensation plans for sales practitioners generally include

   three forms of payment: .... , ... and ....

5. Leveraged sales plans emphasize the payment of commissions.
$$\text{True/False}$$

6. Compensation plans will disclose:
   ❏ When you must deliver a sale.
   ❏ The rules which determine when you are paid for a sale.
   ❏ How much entertainment and travel you can do.
   ❏ The company benefit plan.

7. It is a good business practice to review the sales compensation plan with each individual salesperson. True /False

8. A business that has limited cash resources often wants to offer plans heavily weighted to commissions. True/False

9. Most businesses and sales managers over-assign quota. True/False

10. Different sales assignments will carry different quotas. True/False

CHAPTER 13

Powerful Sales Meetings

Sales Meetings are an integral part of the sales management assignment. You will conduct sales meetings and frequently participate in sales events. The best sales managers quickly learn to make the meetings and events they sponsor and attend highly productive.

Sales meetings should be forums for managers to demonstrate leadership, which features teaching, learning, and motivation. Round out the itinerary with some fun and community building. The agendas must be well-thought out and organized to respect everyone's limited selling time. Well-run sales events inspire teams to perform and achieve, so their value extends beyond the close of the actual program.

Leadership is important to a sales team. Managers expect sales practitioners to lead their prospects as they select products and the company who will be trusted with their business. Ironically, salespeople want leaders as sales managers—people of vision, fortitude and competence to set the direction the sales team will follow. The team also wants managers who speak with clarity and engage in honest discourse.

Sales meetings allow managers to assure their followers that they have a plan and the ability to execute. "Here is where we are...and this is where we're going!" Spend some time discussing the why, how and the who-will-do's of the plan, and you have a winning message.

Learning as a team and individually should take place at each sales meeting or event. As a sales manager, you want to learn what your sales people are experiencing, observing and encountering in their daily selling. What are the prospects saying? Are the customers satisfied? How are people responding to our messages and value propositions?

You also want your sales team to learn what their peers are seeing, saying and experiencing. The power of exposure to other people's observations can be very significant for every person at the sales meeting. I can't recount how many times sales representatives have told me how much they enjoyed sharing their experiences with colleagues and vice-versa.

Use your sales meeting to teach! The audience should be presented with sales skill training, product information, competitive updates and marketing strategy. Any issue which is impacting performance, either positively or negatively, is a topic you want to put on your teaching agenda.

Be certain the teaching and learning extend beyond the sales organization. Sales meetings are company forums, every part of your business should participate. Manufacturing, finance, operations all can learn and teach at these events. When a couple of hundred salespeople tell the head of finance his or her policies are not working or that they are really helping...I can assure you it has a major impact! Every executive in your business needs to have a sales role, and this is a perfect forum to start them on their way.

Sales meetings either motivate your team to greater performance and achievement, or the meeting has failed! As a sales manager, you are the chief motivator in charge. Your performance at the meeting needs to convey a positive message delivered with passion and commitment. Every person on your team will look to you and listen carefully to your comments. They want to be assured you truly believe in the goals you are asking them to accomplish.

Motivation in sales goes hand-in-hand with recognition and awards. You want your salespeople to see and hear success stories and be recognized for their own accomplishments. Nothing is a more powerful motivator than watching your peers win well-deserved accolades!

Sales representatives can experience a sense of isolation, especially those who travel extensively or work from home and remote sales offices. The sales meeting becomes an opportunity to spend time with others experiencing the same challenges. It is comforting to interact with colleagues who truly understand the meaning of "been there and tried that!"

Why are countless sales meetings viewed as a waste of time? How come so many salespeople roll their eyes in dismay when a meeting is announced? The two culprits in my experience are sales managers who fail to plan the events effectively and lack the skills or desire to create powerful meetings. Perhaps in a larger sense, they lack the confidence to expose themselves to the opportunities that a powerful sales meeting presents.

What makes sales meetings powerful?
Planning
Great sales meetings start with careful planning and preparation. The planning requirement is equally valid for large productions as well as smaller meetings. Ask yourself, 'Why are we doing this meeting? What do we need to accomplish?' and then, 'How do we put the event together?'

Targeted agenda
Don't do a sales meeting without preparing an agenda. This simple act forces you to think about what you want to accomplish and makes you

manage the time you have allocated. The more collaboration the agenda reflects, the better it will become! Topics that are important to you should be supplemented with issues the sales team wants to examine and discuss.

A core message

This is the central theme of the sales meeting and the primary reason to convene. "We need to improve our prospecting", "Closing new business seems to be a challenge", "Keep the momentum going by..." are sample messages you build sales meetings and agendas around.

If you don't have a core message, save everybody's selling time and don't hold the meeting; instead, send an e-mail or a note to the team with your news updates and reminders. The worst sales meetings are those in which nothing important is discussed and no real agenda exists.

Communication skills

Sales meetings will test your communication skills! People will listen, react and question. The questions will often test your mettle and patience. The audience will decide if you are serious, committed or just playing games. They will dissect your reasoning and in time will come to know who you are and what matters.

Sales management is leadership—sales meetings are an important stage to help display those leadership skills and qualities. Plain-spoken, sincere and reasoned are three qualities that will help you communicate. In my experience, sales managers who are communication-challenged really struggle with sales meetings. Just remember, the more sales meetings you conduct, the more comfortable you will become with the platform. If your communications skills are an issue, find classes, coaches and books that can help you strengthen this crucial talent!

Execution

Crisp, well-run meetings send a positive message to salespeople. The agenda is followed, presentations get done and the meeting respects every participant's time. The event is viewed as productive and well-organized, qualities business people respect.

The sales managers I worked for who had poor organizational skills ran disastrous sales meetings. They often started and finished late, had non-existent rambling agendas, featured speakers and other guests who failed to show, and wasted a lot of valuable selling time. The whole exercise seem to be in a constant state of commotion! Your sales team deserves a well-executed sales meeting—it demonstrates leadership and respect for their time and yours.

Follow-up

Very few sales meetings finish without a list of items for follow-up. Powerful sales meetings are evidenced by managers delivering answers to the open items! If an issue was important enough to commit to getting an answer for, then it deserves closure.

Simple e-mails or text messages, sent within a couple of business days, can be used to close most of the items listed for follow-up. Open items not resolved before the next sales meeting should be placed on the subsequent meeting's agenda for final disposition.

Karen Dunlop awoke to a fuzzy head—just another bout of jet lag. In the four years that had passed, she commuted between the old AG headquarters in Frankfurt, Germany, and the Midwest the way millions of commuters ride the subway to work. Despite her efforts, the jet lag never quite went away.

"This is going to be a two shot of espresso start," she assured herself. "Today, I have to be at my best, the annual sales kickoff is big. I need my best performance...get the team motivated to break last year's records."

The phone rang, "Good morning, Karen." Helen Black, the VP of Marketing was taking no chances—she wanted her boss up early and in the zone for the sales event of the year. "Well, today we wow them with your presentation. Do you realize how much work has gone into this meeting? We started the planning three months ago, remember? The PowerPoints are superb. I rehearsed everyone's presentation except Kelly's. I'm sure he will do fine...I can't make him stick to a script anyway...!"

"Thanks, Helen, I'm going to hit the shower and I'll be in by 8."

The organization that went into the event was time-consuming, but the payoff was critical. Four years of record sales and the flawless integration of AG had taught Karen the importance of teamwork, planning and execution. Her promotion to Executive Vice President last year had moved her further from daily sales life and deeper into the business strategy challenge.

"At least today, for the whole day, I get to be around all our sales people and learn from them. They also need to hear my message for this new year...and take it to heart." Karen stared at the empty parking space. "Did I leave my car somewhere?"

"Karen!" Robert's voice pierced her fog.

"Sorry, I gave the Benz to Cuddyer. He had some visitors in from China and wanted to impress them..."

Karen shook her head in relief, "That's fine. I just thought I lost

175

the car somehow. I'm glad to hear someone else is using it!"

Robert grabbed her briefcase and opened the car door.

"What are you doing here?"

"Well, I wasn't going to let you walk to work. Besides, I needed to go over the details of the budget projections for Asia and Europe. We also have a couple of sales contracts with some addendums you are going to have to approve."

Robert may have been a marginal sales manager, but he had become an exceptional administrator. The AG sales integration was testimony to his ability to grasp details and never miss a piece of minutia. Even the skeptical Germans were in awe of his talent to make things run on schedule.

"I just want you to know how much I value what you do!"

"Stop...you're making me blush. I'm just glad you chose to forget how bad a sales manager I was."

"You were not bad, you just needed more experience!'

"Okay, thanks!"

"Your opening speech has been extended by 15 minutes to give you time to take some extra questions. I know the salespeople will really like that. You seem to enjoy the format and it shows."

"Great!"

"By the way, Bob will be the featured lunch speaker, he has several announcements to make. Then you and he will take audience questions."

"I haven't talked to Bob this week." Just then her cell phone rang...Bob Kelly.

"Karen, welcome back! I just want you to be the first to know—I signed your deal to acquire Triad Press Ltd., so Cuddyer will have himself a great customer base in Asia. Be sure you mention that in your opening speech. Patti has all the details...see you later!" and he was gone.

Robert handed her a two page document. "I fixed your PowerPoints. The first page is the press release, the talking points are on page two. Patti Scarzo will take you through any details you need. We didn't want to call you last night."

Karen scanned the documents.

"Patti and Cuddyer are leaving for Singapore after the meeting...you okay for going?"

"I guess I am."

The car pulled up to the front door and Don Brown, VP-North American Sales, opened the door. "Hey boss...welcome home! You need some coffee..."

The adrenaline rush kicked in when she stepped onto the stage. Butterflies and the chill of anticipation...

176

"Good morning! It's a pleasure to be in the company of the best sales team in the business. The bright, hard-working sales professionals who have achieved...yet another record performance. You are simply amazing! Because you have broken all records, Robert and his team have also broken a record...Rather than wait several weeks to receive your year- end bonuses and commissions, you'll get them this very moment!"

The room erupted into applause and cheers. Karen was on cue, on message, and, like most effective speakers, making all the attention to detail and practice appear spontaneous and unscripted. When the room quieted down, she began to teach.

"Professionals recognize they can and must do better—amateurs try to rest on their laurels. Our challenge this year is to accelerate the replacement of our older presses with our new models. Why? First, it's in our customers' best financial interest; and secondly, it is in our interest to solidify our market leadership position while our competitors are pre-occupied with their own challenges. The new presses will secure our accounts for years to come...and lock our competitors out! We are going to offer trade-in allowances and financing which will make it difficult for anyone not to accept our proposals!"

Applause and cheers.

"For this strategy to work, you need to spend more face time with our existing clients. The calls we make on current customers have to increase by a factor of three. I know you will do this because it is the right thing to do! But, to focus your attention, the new sales compensation plan will offer the opportunity to earn higher commission rates and bonuses for every conversion you sell!"

She let the audience take in her lesson and then slipped into the learning mode. "I'd like to hear from you: What are we doing that's work-ing? What should we be doing to help you be more successful?"

The first questioner jumped to his feet and took the microphone, "Karen, the reason many of us have not really asked the customers to replace their current presses—and I'm not being negative—the SC6000 is still...well...it's suspect as a reliable unit. We keep making this point and I don't know if it is getting through!"

"We did have some early units with problems but I believe that is behind us. Let's have Sydney address your question after her Engineering presentation this morning."

The questions kept coming.

"Why can't marketing do a better job of...?"

"We need more service engineers in my territory!"

"I would like to know if it is possible to...?"

She treated each question and person with sincerity and respect.

177

Each topic was noted and either scheduled for more discussion or resolved on the spot.

"What about Triad? They're becoming a serious competitive threat in my territory."

"Really?"

"They are...a problem. Good presses and very inexpensive. They appeal to a niche in our market."

Karen could barely contain her glee...she paused for a moment and turned to motivation. "Baker Industries is a unique business. I feel privileged to work with so many fine people who are so committed to being first and foremost the leader in this market. Look around the room at our management team: Bob Kelly, our CEO and Founder, a sales executive! Helen Black, VP of Marketing, a sales executive! Patti Scarzo, VP of Business Development, a sales executive! Don Brown, VP of Sales, a sales executive! Smitty, a sales executive. I started as a sales director, Robert started as a sales director! We are a sales-driven company, and I say that without any apologies to anyone. How many of the 300 salespeople in this room earned a six-figure salary last year? Please stand up!"

The room seemed to rise as one.

"210 of our best salespeople to be exact! Why? Because as a sales-driven company, we demand and then reward real performance! It's clear to me you are up to accepting this challenge once again this year."

The energy in the room was palpable.

"You asked about Triad? They were a great competitor, they had great products. I said 'were' and 'had' intentionally. You see, as a sales-driven company we are attuned to our competitors, we respect them and then we buy them! Yes..." waving a press release. "Yes, as of 9 a.m. this morning, Triad has become the Pacific Rim Division of Baker Industries! James Scott Cuddyer, a sales executive, will become the General Manager of the Division."

With that, Karen thanked her audience and made one final remark. "Everyone in this room has the power within to seize your greatest dreams and ambitions, it will be my privilege to help you do just that!" She left the stage.

Bob Kelly spoke first at the luncheon. "After listening to Karen this morning, I'm seriously thinking about going back to carrying a bag and just plain selling! The first day I had the opportunity to listen to Karen speak, I told Smitty she was a 'Gardener'...someone who made the people around her grow and be better than they were or even believed they could be. She has worked tirelessly for all of us." He stopped, pointed to her and led the applause.

"So now I am going to ask yet one more thing of her, because I know she will excel in this new assignment and it's a task which is crucial to our company's future."

Helen Black interrupted Karen's side conversation with Don Brown and whispered, "You may want to pay attention to this part."

Kelly plunged ahead..."It is time for me to turn my attention to issues beyond the daily operations of this company. I feel the transition period we have gone through for the last several years is over, and personally, I don't need to be running the business. Thank God! But the President of Baker Industries should be someone who understands the culture of a sales-driven business—a Sales Executive! That person is here and is already in charge, it's time for me to step aside and let Karen Dunlop officially lead this business!"

Helen screamed, "Yes! I knew it!"

Karen sat speechless for a long moment.

TEST YOUR KNOWLEDGE

1. Don't conduct a sales meeting without preparing an agenda.

    True/False

2. What makes a sales meeting powerful?
    - ❏ A targeted agenda.
    - ❏ A core message.
    - ❏ Crisp execution.
    - ❏ All the above.

3. Very few sales meetings finish without a list of items for follow-up.

    True/False

4. Sales meetings are a venue to expose the entire company to the challenges a sales team is encountering.   True/False

5. Sales meetings should feature...
    - ❏ Teaching.
    - ❏ Learning.
    - ❏ Motivation.
    - ❏ All of the above.

6. The sales meeting is an opportunity for salespeople to spend time with others experiencing the same challenges.   True/False

7. The worst sales meetings are those in which nothing important is discussed and no real agenda exists.   True/False

8. Participating in sales meetings should be restricted to those who work in the sales department.   True/False

9. Sales meetings are an ideal time to present awards recognizing extraordinary achievements.   True/False

10. Sales meetings will test your communications skills!   True/False

All Sales Managers Have Four Constituencies

The Four Constituencies Are:

Salespeople—the core audience all sales managers must lead, manage and challenge to achievement.
Your personal success is the result of the performance of your sales team! The sales managers who choose to minimize their involvement with this constituency, or who dismiss sales practitioners as the foundation of their assignment, don't succeed!

Colleagues—the people with whom you work.
They are not part of the sales organization but are interrelated. You will need their cooperation, assistance and support in order to accomplish your mission. Your ability to win their confidence and create positive working relationships will have a direct impact on your sales team. Colleagues can roll up their sleeves and help make a salesforce successful or fight your efforts every step of the way!

Executive Management—your supervisor and the other senior executives in your business.
The executive team has to understand and support the sales assignment. They can help you find and solicit new business opportunities and open doors for your salespeople. The more involved and supportive they are, the better your chances for success will become. It's your job to make them full partners and participants in the sales agenda!

Customers and Prospects—those who buy your products and services.

This is an audience from which you need to learn and, just as important- ly, needs to learn from you! Sales managers need a clear vision of what their prospects and customers are thinking. How are they are reacting to your proposals, products, competitors and the greater marketplace? You learn as you interact with this constituency! This knowledge can be shared with your salespeople, colleagues, and executive managers, so the business can make smart market-driven decisions.

Prospects in turn learn about your business, its products and your future plans from meeting salespeople and their managers. Relationships are built by sharing information and developing common interests. Successful sales managers are always actively involved with this crucial group.

 Bob Kelly proposed a first toast to the new President of Baker Industries.

"Shouldn't we at least wait for Karen?" Robert asked.

"I told her to get a nap and we would let her catch up to us at din- ner. It's my job to be sure we take care of her."

Somewhere between the second and third round Helen asked her question, "Bob, when did you decide Karen was ready to run the business? How did you decide?"

"I can't say when I decided—it was a while ago. I knew it was the right thing to do after I was certain she had satisfied four constituencies."

"What?"

"The four groups of people all sales managers need to win over."

Helen stared intensely and then smiled. "I'm not sure if this is a Kelly moment or the start of a bad joke, but tell me, just who are these people?"

"First on the list were the salespeople, that was easy because I was enjoying a third or fourth career as a salesperson when she joined the company. Al hired her, so I really didn't meet her until she was introduced to our team. It didn't take much of an intellect to see she was a salesper- son's delight: Her people came first, but she also demanded as much as she gave. I always knew where I stood with her, and what she expected from me. She told me once, 'My job is to make you successful; if I do that, my own success will take care of itself.' I watched her hire and fire sales- people, she always treated everybody fairly and with respect. She never did anyone special deals or favors and that included me!"

Sydney Day, the VP of Engineering, spoke next. "Karen and I got off to a rough start as colleagues. Al Winters took her to task for her behavior. She made a conscious choice to apologize for her mistake and then to build a relationship between us. We don't always agree, but she's open-minded and fair. I have come to trust her, plain and simple! She will always have the business's interest first, but she will not use her position to profit personally at another's expense."

The Comptroller volunteered, "She can be a force to be reckoned with. I have a budget officer who will not forget that lesson. In time, I became convinced it was never personal, it was about a sense of doing what she feels is right, she isn't into taking advantage of her peers. Her focus is about doing what's right for the business and people."

"She was tested by executive management on several occasions, especially by Dan at his infamous forecast summit. He pushed Norton who folded; but Karen rose to the occasion, showed good judgment and the courage of her convictions."

Al Winters continued, "Karen never ceased to surprise me. I knew when I hired her she grasped what sales managers must do to succeed. What I never expected was how fast she would build a team, how strong her leadership skills were and what a quick study she was. She was a better sales manager during her first year than I ever was!"

The VP of Marketing shook his head, "Al, you missed her best quality! She knows how to listen and to learn. I don't think she much cares who she learns from, her mind is open and curious. The curiosity feeds on itself and it makes her so engaging to deal with."

Kelly volunteered, "The prospects certainly like dealing with her. What you consistently hear is her being described as—personable, but no push-over; a smart negotiator who knows what she wants; is willing to make fair compromises, but never fails to meet commitments. Karen understands long-term relationships matter to our business and its customers, she has invested her time and effort in cultivating them."

Smitty couldn't resist, "Taking shortcuts to close deals never seemed to be of much interest to her, and over the years, I have come to respect this greatly."

Professional sales managers have four constituencies that they must cultivate, nuture and effect. The sales team is their first and foremost focus of attention. However, they never forget to manage up the organization and to reach across the business to engage their peers. The care of customers and prospects is essential...for without this body, the business itself is non-existent! Balancing and responding to the needs of each constituency is what makes them true professionals.

TEST YOUR KNOWLEDGE

1. Name the four constituencies each sales manager must serve.

    1. ....

    2. ....

    3. ....

    4. ....

2. Describe why each constituency is important.

....

....

....

....

PART II

SALES MANAGEMENT ASSIGNMENTS

The Transition
To
Sales Management

I chose the word 'transition' for this chapter because it conveys a passage. In Latin, it means 'to go across'. Sales people who become sales managers will find both terms accurately describe their experience. Perhaps the best description of the transition came from a savvy friend who used the following line to describe life as a sales manager:

The highs are not as high—the lows are not as low! You get held accountable for your own performance and everyone else's.

I actually found his words contained real wisdom; they were valid from the first to the last day I served as a sales manager. I can assure you being a sales manager is quite different from working as a salesperson.

Managers and individual contributors

The essential difference between sales and sales management is the transition from individual contributor to manager! Your personal success is now judged by the performance and achievement of your sales team. You will quickly discover you can no longer rely on just your personal sales skills and acumen.

Working through others and leading a team to achievement requires a new and expanded set of skills and a different mindset! It is why many excellent sales practitioners struggle with the transition. An examination of the noun 'management' in any dictionary will give you a taste of the reality to come: administration, charge, care, direction, leadership, control, governing, rule, command, supervision, overseeing, guidance and operation. Sales representatives must master a lengthy portfolio of new skills as they transition to management.

The mindset shift begins with your commitment to make the people who work for you the focus of your effort and attention. Their success comes first and foremost, and you constantly act for their benefit.

When you work through other people you also become responsible for their mistakes and failings. Teaching a sales team how to 'do it right every time' can be a wonderful experience or a frustrating exercise. In time you come to understand, whatever results a team delivers—they belong to you! Sales managers are judged by the performance of others, which is very different from how individual contributors are valued.

Changing constituencies

We just finished a discussion about the audiences sales managers must affect and serve. Sales representatives primarily focus on prospects and customers. Managers start with their sales team! Salespeople interact with executive managers and colleagues, they sell both externally and internally. However, the selling is primarily at a transactional level—they ask for help with particular deals. Sales managers interact at broader and more strategic levels and the audience's support and cooperation is often more challenging both to secure initially and to keep.

I have heard time and again new managers confess they misjudged the complexity, importance and challenge of their audiences."When I was in sales and needed help, it was easy to persuade people to get involved. No one wanted to be responsible for losing a sales for me! When I became a sales manager, the relationships became more complicated, just the threat of losing a sale no longer got the immediate results I wanted."

Managers are not always appreciated
Perhaps you always held your sales managers in great esteem. Here's a flash...not all salespeople do! Sometimes for good reasons, and occasionally for absolutely no reason, you will not be greeted with open arms by an audience waiting for leadership and guidance. The hostile, skeptical or indifferent reception may extend to several or all of your constituencies.

I have experienced managing sales teams who literally rolled out a welcome mat and those who didn't want to acknowledge my presence. Unfortunately, transitions can become a true test of wills or a trial-by-fire.

It's important to select your first sales management assignment with care. The culture of the business and the existing sales organization can and will have a material impact on your success. Don't hesitate to explore this issue when you interview! Ask your potential managers, colleagues and the sales team members if and how they will assist you in making a successful transition. Get any challenges or reservations on the table and discuss them thoroughly.

> *One of my most rewarding assignments began when the CEO of the company where I was interviewing quickly told me how dysfunctional his sales team was. "You can fire them all...or I'll do it for you!" He made certain we had a plan to reshape the salesforce from the first day.*
>
> *I learned in time his emotions sometimes got the best of him, but his candor and unswerving support made for a long and successful relationship. Incidentally, I removed very few of his sales representatives because we determined the key issue inhibiting their performance was motivation. We also concluded, personalities aside, the business could not succeed with a lot of unfilled sales territories!*

During an elaborate sales awards ceremony honoring many members of my sales team, someone asked me this question, "Why do they always give the best awards and most accolades to the salespeople and not to the sales managers?" My answer was simple, accurate and honest, "They did the work, my job was to make it possible."

Entry-level management assignments

Entry assignments are often restrictive in their scope and assigned responsibilities. In many businesses and industries, the career path to a coveted Vice President of Sales position may include a number of intermediate sales management jobs and countless years of experience.

Managing small teams on a short leash with very restricted authority can be difficult for individual contributors who have grown accustomed to independently working their own territories and accounts. It is often viewed as an unpleasant and difficult career choice.

Unfortunately, every new sales manager, even a seasoned salesman or woman, needs to start someplace! Entry-level assignments are a controlled way to allow growth in stature and competency without completely jeopardizing an employer's revenue plan. Much like you did as a new sales practitioner, use the opportunity to learn and then refine your skills. In time, you will either be given greater responsibility or decide to take your career in another direction. The employer who first gives you a management opportunity may be only one of many stops in your career journey. Sales management experience is valuable...plain and simple!

The financials

Top sales representatives earn more than most sales managers! Why? Salespeople ultimately close business transactions. The compensation rewards go to those who take the most risk and bear the burden of direct and final responsibility for revenue creation.

Sales managers can and will occasionally close a sale, but it's the sales representatives who either succeed or fail to master this important step in the sales methodology. Managers are directly compensated for the sales their team achieves. Since the team's performance determines its manager's compensation, sales managers who want to make money should start by focusing on the results their team produces.

If your sales strategy, coaching, leadership, and motivation skills make a positive difference, the results will shine through...as sales! If your team fails, then you also will suffer financially. The transition includes making some financial adjustments and occasional sacrifices.

The results and accountability

Much like sales practitioners, managers are judged on the results they deliver. I want to dispel any thoughts that sales managers are somehow more secure in their jobs than salespeople. The assignments are different, but being in management is not a respite from either the demand to perform or the need. The simple reality is you will exchange an individual quota for a larger team-dependent revenue plan.

When results disappoint, it may be easier to remove the manager than it is to replace an entire sales team. Sales management is not a place to hide or retire! I marvel at the number of new sales managers who somehow feel they are exempt from accountability. "My salespeople have a problem, I don't!" is an illogical statement. The idea that a manager can succeed while the team fails—is wrong. More often than not this painful lesson will be quickly delivered by your constituencies!

Fast starts matter

The quicker you take charge of your team the better! Why? The honeymoon effect is in play. The decision to recruit a new sales manager is always preceded by relief in accomplishing the task. Once the sales manager is on board, the collective stage is set to address other important sales or business issues. Even if the team you inherit is successful, the business will expect positive changes...which is exactly why you were hired!

The longer it takes you to engage, the quicker your honeymoon capital dissipates and the greater your association with the status quo becomes. New managers often are uncertain about the limits of their authority and how much change they can effect—the quicker you test those limits, the better!

Engage each of your audiences, roll up your sleeves, get involved with the sales team and start to unravel the challenges which are inhibiting their achievement. The sales teams, and every other constituency, want to see leadership...now rather than later!

Succeeding In Your First Assignment

Many sales managers struggle and fail in the first management assignment they attempt. Some will fail several times. I believe you can do better! It is just as easy to succeed as it is to fail and the experience is far more pleasant.

First assignments come in two initial forms, both of which we shall discuss in detail. For clarity we will define 'Successful Teams' as those who have made their annual revenue plan and 'Failing Teams' as those who have missed plan. Success and failure come in many gradients, missing a sales goal by 10% is less serious than a 50% shortfall, but we'll keep our discussions in the broadest forms.
- Managing a successful team
- Managing a failing team

In both cases, a new manager is asked to move a sales team forward, one to greater levels of performance, the other to an acceptable measure of achievement. The challenges are similar and yet different.

Managing a successful team
It may come as a surprise but managing a successful team can be a more difficult assignment than dealing with a failing organization. Success in sales can be more difficult to sustain than to achieve! Why? Because of human nature. Some people handle success positively and use what they have accomplished to push themselves to greater achievements. They remind themselves, "I can perform even better if I continue to learn and work smarter and harder!"

Unfortunately, others experience success and quickly stop doing the very things that made them successful! "I'm a star so I don't have to do all those things I disliked doing!"

Sometimes salespeople are just plain lucky. Their performance is driven by outside forces which have little to do with selling skills or discipline. The good fortune runs its course and the bottom falls out.

Sales teams and selling environments are dynamic. Representatives come and go, products evolve, markets shift and realign. Businesses gain and lose momentum to existing competitors. New players enter markets, economic conditions change. Companies and the constituencies within can fundamentally be changed by success, for the better or worse. What worked yesterday is history—what sells tomorrow is often an unknown.
The team you inherit may be fundamentally different from the entity that achieved its plan!

196

I managed a sales team for several years which broke every goal and revenue plan they were presented. Everyone literally achieved plan! And then the bottom fell out. The market shifted and orders that had been routinely placed became a struggle to earn. Company executives were slow to respond to the new environment, they spent months arguing and generally refusing to accept reality. The sales representatives were in shock! The order takers floundered and failed.

The true sales professionals adjusted and began executing the selling skills demanded by a difficult business climate. One of my star salesmen commented, "I've gone from shooting fish in a barrel to doing real selling!"

Managers who inherit successful teams are placed under scrutiny when sales results stall or falter. The only acceptable outcome for the new leaders of previously successful teams is...to deliver greater achievements! You manage to the future with its opportunities and challenges and don't rely on what happened last year or last quarter.

When you are asked to manage a successful sales team, approach the assignment with the cautious optimism it deserves. The achievements may not be as clear-cut as they appear and the challenge of doing more is real. Finally, keep in mind that your team's history, despite its comforting record, is not a guarantee of your future performance.

Managing a failing team
Inheriting a failed effort certainly provides you with a clear mission—make it successful! It typically comes with the challenge of figuring out exactly what has to be done to restart the sales engine. What it rarely includes is the luxury of time. The demand for results will be both clear and immediate and the plea will come from each of your constituencies. The more serious the sales shortfall, the more urgent the turn-around.

Failing teams present new managers with several opportunities. First, you will get visibility and plenty of organizational cooperation. Second, even the most minor signs of progress will be well-received; and when you finally succeed, the event will be celebrated and rewarded! Businesses experiencing sales failures are often desperate for a leader who can return the revenue stream to healthy performance levels.

The challenge of inheriting a failing sales team is twofold. You will have a limited window of time and the risk that the sales problem is beyond your ability or that of the organization's to resolve. Revenue failures are not always rooted in the sales team. Try selling a product that doesn't work or has a poor performance history, and you'll quickly understand my point. Businesses that can't sell their products or their services are destined to

197

disappear and everyone associated with the effort will share in the failure.

The opportunity for managerial success is not materially impacted by inheriting a successful team instead of a failing one! Teams that have a record of achievement need to be approached with cautious optimism. Underperforming sales organizations should be carefully scrutinized to be certain the challenge they present is a sales question. First time sales managers need to restrict the challenges they face to sales-concentric issues, rather than broader business problems.

Whatever sales team you choose, you need to get off to a fast start. In fact, it's imperative! Our **Fast Start Plan** has served me well in a multitude of difficult sales management assignments. I am confident you will find it invaluable and come to appreciate its importance!

The Fast Start Plan for Sales Managers

- ☑ Due Diligence is Critical
- ☑ Homework Starts Long Before Day One
- ☑ Leadership Begins Immediately
- ☑ Interview Each Salesperson
- ☑ Communicate Your Goals and Expectations
- ☑ Listen and Learn!
- ☑ Decisions Drive Motivation
- ☑ Watch Them Sell
- ☑ Account Management Plans and Forecasts Are Required!
- ☑ Recruit and Terminate—Build a Team

Due diligence is critical

Accept only positions where you believe you will succeed! The smartest way to prevent the disappointment of failure is to be selective and careful about the positions you accept. Invest your time and effort in performing due diligence about potential employers before you interview and after they extend an employment offer.

Every business hiring a sales manager has a reason for the action. It's important for you to understand why they are hiring and the real circumstances leading to the decision. Was someone promoted? Were they terminated? Why? How did the sales team perform? Did they make plan or miss? Keep asking these important questions during the interview process.

Ask your employer how they intend to help you succeed at your first sales management assignment...and listen carefully. You want to work for companies and individuals who have a vested interest in your success. They will express a commitment to helping you succeed because the assignment is too important to allow you to fail!

The reason for due diligence is—some assignments are impossible. The plan is too aggressive, the product is late, the business is dysfunctional, a list of insurmountable challenges too long to do justice to! Savvy sales managers learn from first-hand experience that some assignments fail the risk vs. reward test. The sales challenge is so significant and so systemic that it is beyond successful resolution by a mere mortal.

The mere fact you were offered an opportunity is not a reason to accept. A business struggling for sales revenue will make decisions based on wishes and promises they somehow justify as reasonable. Unfortunately, sales managers are sometimes set-up to fail by their own supervisors, people who want to escape accountability by making the sales problem yours alone.

Early in my career, I interviewed for a senior sales director's position with the VP of Sales at a very trendy competitor. The more I learned about this individual, the more skeptical I became about the position.

During our interview, he regaled in telling me how he had fired the last three incumbents who held the now open manager's position. When I asked him if he had made plan, he went immediately into blame mode. The incompetence of his sales directors had prevented him from achieving plan—it was all their fault! Try as I did, I could not get an explanation of how the sales revenue target was derived or what planning exercise was behind the quota. Nothing! He asked me if I was up to this challenging assignment? I responded with a question of my own. "Do you want me to make plan or are you looking for another scapegoat?" His face turned red. I leaned forward and told him, "Look, I have better things to do than volunteer to be Failure #4." So ended our interview.

Unfortunately, a colleague of mine happily accepted the offer and became victim #4 in six short months!

Choose the opportunities that offer personal commitments and well-thought-out plans to assist you in meeting expectations.

Homework starts long before day one
Before your official first day, you should become acquainted with every salesperson on your team, their performance records and resumes. If the team is too large or too geographically disbursed, focus on learning about the key contributors.

Try to meet as many salespeople as you can during the interview process. Ask the same kind of open-ended questions you would pose to any prospect or customer. Let them share their opinions, observations and anything else they deem important. If you listen, the amount of information you will be exposed to will positively surprise and delight! This knowledge will help you get organized, set goals, plan and make important decisions early in your tenure.

The same logic applies to colleagues, the better you know them and what matters from their perspective—the quicker your start!

Leadership begins immediately
The first several days should send a clear message about the type of leadership you will provide. I want you to be visible, active and fully engaged in learning, absorbing information and making decisions. No one on the team should doubt for a moment your personal commitment to setting new performance standards and helping each sales representative excel. The worst thing you can do is disappear or be locked in meetings and conferences which make your presence a mystery to the salesforce.

The sales team is your primary audience in the critical early going. Remind your other constituencies of this simple fact: "I need to get my hands around the sales organization!"

The best advice I can give you about being a leader is a reminder that 'Leaders have followers.' They work to be sure their followers are successful, their own success comes from the accomplishments of others.

Interview each salesperson

I refer to this as a get acquainted exercise—best done in person, in private and casually. The intent is to start building relationships and discussing what help they need and how you like to work.

Don't be afraid to talk about your background, things you enjoy and your plans for the sales team. Listen to what is important to them; the things they like and appreciate or don't particularly enjoy. Suggestions, criticism, praise and disapproval are all fair game and welcomed. This introductory meeting is the prelude to a more formal discussion of the individual performance expectations you will require.

Communicate your goals and expectations

Within the first week, hold a sales meeting to lay out the goals you are going to pursue—sales growth, new compensation plans, territory changes, shifts of product strategies, the resolution of specific challenges and bottlenecks. Articulate what you're going to accomplish and why! Focus on the importance of measurable sales results and your commitment to help everyone achieve plan.

The goals may be revised or adjusted as you gain a better understanding of the scope of your assignment, but the sales team needs to know your leadership is at hand!

Listen and learn!

The more input you receive, the greater your knowledge base. Keep an open mind and expose your curiosity to opinions and suggestions. Judge what is valuable and what should be discarded.

The sales team will appreciate your willingness to listen. They will not expect you to accept or act on every idea. The exercise is valuable because it will assist you in evaluating what's in play with the salesforce and who is thinking about particular issues. It will also allow you to discover the thought leaders and wisdom sources within the team.

Decisions drive motivation

Making quick decisions will motivate your team. Leaders don't avoid making decisions! I'm not advocating reckless behavior. However, I will argue that waiting months to make even basic decisions is reckless and happens far too often. Don't be afraid to change things that aren't working and serve no valuable purpose. Your team will lead you right to the door of these problems and it's your job to open that door.

I have been told many times, "I don't know if the decision you've made is 100% correct, but the fact you did something about the issue is incredible!" Decisions can always be re-worked and refined, doing nothing has a way of becoming a legacy.

Every sales organization will respond to the removal of obstacles that inhibit performance. Failed policies, senseless paperwork and sales prevention rules are often drags on a team's motivation. When you dispose of these problems, the message you send is clear...we are moving ahead!

Watch them sell

Nothing will tell you more about the skills each salesperson possesses than watching them sell. The sooner you observe them in action, the quicker you will know who is a star and who is mediocre or worse. You'll also learn what coaching and training needs are most crucial to improving their individual performance.

Some salespeople are much better at selling to their managers than to prospects. I have always been surprised to discover how good (or how terrible) some of my salespeople really were in front of real prospects and customers. I learned in time to assume nothing—just observe them live and in action!

Account management plans and forecasts are required!

Spend time in your second week going through each salesperson's key accounts and current forecast. It will help you discover if the team has any standardized approach to account management plans or forecasting.

This is the ideal opportunity to make it clear what specific results you want them to deliver. "I expect you to close these three accounts by quarter's end and make your plan of $500,000. If you can't do this, I need to understand why."

The exercise will also provide insight into how each person manages a sale or if they simply improvise each deal. Top performers have standardized methodologies they use to manage each prospect, from qualification to closing, step by step. If they are unprepared, they get to come back and re-do the exercise in 24 hours. The message of the importance you place on account management and forecasting will be communicated very quickly!

Recruit and terminate—build a team

Within several short weeks, you will be able to begin the process of building out your sales team. The organization's 'keepers' will be apparent, those 'on-the-bubble' should get the benefit of more attention, and the sales representatives you feel need to be replaced should be given performance plans and placed on probation. Occasionally, a team has one or two members who are performing poorly or have lost interest in participating. They often expect to be cut but will wait for management to take the initiative.

I remember a salesperson, who had gone many months without making a sale, coming into my office for our first get-acquainted meeting. He was polite and seemed to be very intelligent. I asked why he had performed so poorly and he replied, "I'm not much of a salesperson, I should never have taken the job. It's not very interesting work." I inquired, "Why are you still working here?" He volunteered, "Well, it pays my bills, the coffee is free and no one else seems to care!" I then asked, "So, what do you suggest we do?" The answer..."Well, Tom, if I were you—I would fire me." And I did.

The best approach is to remove the obvious failures quickly, so there are no questions about your willingness to address the difficult personnel decisions. And, the sooner you replace employees who can't or will not contribute, the quicker you can get people in place who share your vision—those who truly want the opportunity to grow professionally and succeed!

The reason so many new managers fail in their first assignment is that they stumble out of the gate because of inexperience and cautious behavior. Indecision sends a message to the selling team that the status-quo is being extended indefinitely. The audience tunes out and moves on, never giving you the chance to correct this lackluster first impression.

You can greatly increase the opportunity for success in the opening weeks of an assignment with a fast start! Your new followers want the fresh leadership and vision which accompanies a fast start. You only get one 'first' chance to move a team forward...make the most of it!

Sales Managers Without Sales Experience

In an ideal world, sales managers possess expertise in sales and management. The majority of professional sales managers start as salespeople and then learn to manage. Some (like this author) start as managers, work as salespeople and return as sales managers. Every so often, a manager becomes a sales manager without any sales experience. Unusual? Yes! Challenging? Definitely!

It was a wonderful late summer afternoon in New England, crisp clear sky...and traffic! Cars and trucks as far as the eye could see...crawling towards the Thomas Callahan Tunnel, the gateway to Boston's own Logan Airport...were all that stood between me and a well-deserved weekend at the lake. Jeff, my current sales manager, was fidgeting in the passenger seat.

It was my first return to sales after electing to take a break from sales management. I missed the camaraderie of managing a team, but I was enjoying my newly discovered independence and the joy of just selling. My passenger, on the other hand, was in misery as he clung to the hope he could somehow survive his first year as a sales director.

"Tom, I don't understand how your team made its numbers for the last two years. I'm at 60% and August, the worst month, is about to close. Other than your new sale, I have nothing for the month. Everyone is screaming I messed up this sales team."

I really wanted to avoid this discussion because I hated the thought of honestly telling Jeff he was in over his head, and the end result was very predictable! So...I tried to feign surprise. "Listen, the team you have today is different from the one I had. You lost several top performers and the economy is going into recession. It's like trying to compare apples and oranges."

Silence and..."You never wanted me get this job, did you? I know you weren't crazy about my not having any sales experience and coming directly from a product management position. I'm not a salesperson..."

The car was becoming increasingly small. It was time to be honest without being hurtful. "This company is not a sales-driven business. It was founded by engineers who liked to invent things. To them, selling has always been a necessary evil. Salespeople have always been suspect... that is why the CEO wanted a product person for the job. Any sales manager would find this assignment difficult! I spent years as a salesman, this was my second sales management assignment, and I had a difficult time! Jeff, your sales inexperience and the culture are working against you. The job is not about product...sorry...it's about selling and management. It's hard to hide from selling when you have ten salespeople!"

The challenge for first-level sales managers without sales experience is leading a team that needs to be coached, taught, motivated and listened to—when much of what they need is foreign to your experience or intellect. The smaller the organization and the more inexperienced the salesforce, the greater the chasm.

It's easier for managers without sales skills to function as a VP of Sales in larger organizations. Why? You can surround yourself with sales managers who provide for the 'hands-on' needs of the salesforce, while you tend to other constituencies. In my first sales management assignment, I worked for exactly that type of VP of Sales. His focus was on customers, colleagues, executive management and his sales directors. He rarely, if ever, interacted with the salesforce; that was my responsibility. Ideal? No, but the business succeeded!

Filling the sales experience void

If you are about to become a sales manager without the benefit of significant sales experience, here are some opportunities and issues to consider:

Talk about your resume

"I don't have any real sales experience. I wish I had had that opportunity, but I am a quick learner and with your help I will get up to speed." Disarm the grumbling before it starts, ask for help! The salesforce will quickly discover you lack experience, so get out in front of the news.

When you are asked why you took the assignment, respond, "Because the company asked me, and I think it's a great opportunity!" Positive attitude, no excuses offered!

The salesforce and selling is the first priority

Get out and make sales calls with your salespeople and on your own. Find a top performer and let him/her mentor you. Set aside several days each month or each week to work with your people as they prospect, qualify, present and close orders. Just roll up your sleeves, participate and learn.

Volunteer to fill-in for salespeople who are sick, on vacation or have schedule conflicts. "Let me handle this call (meeting, presentation) for you." A second set of eyes and ears in competitive sales contests are always appreciated. "Here's what I observed, I think..." You will earn the respect of your team and, in time, their trust.

Conversely, the worst thing you can do is to hide. In the story at the start of this chapter, my sales manager made this very mistake. He felt his lack of experience precluded him from participating in any sales activities. Months went by before he made a single sales call. He never attended a presentation or picked up the phone to call a prospect. Jeff became a sales manager without a sales role! Those types of managers don't survive very long...and neither did Jeff!

Hire experienced sales representatives

Jeff replaced experienced professionals with rookies. He felt less challenged by having sales representatives who had as little experience as he did! Unfortunately, his new practitioners needed large measures of coaching, tutoring and training. When they were unable to get the attention they deserved, they tried to teach themselves and, in time, ran for the exits.

Surround yourself with smart people who can draw from your strengths and reinforce your shortcomings. The more sales experience you can hire, the better your short-term performance will be.

Play to your strengths

Jeff was a product expert. What he should have done was add his expertise to that of his sales team's repertoire of skills! A team is greater than its individual parts, add your expertise to the mix and every team member will benefit.

A sales manager who is an engineer or a accountant can easily add value if he or she crafts a role. Work with your team to create the capacity that best fits your strengths. Some managers are terrific at discussing important business directions with prospects. "I would like to brief you on our company's new business plan, discuss our strategic acquisition program, acquaint you with our new customer service facilities, etc."—information prospects often want to know before they select a vendor. Salespeople can always use assistance in their quest to deliver results, be creative in deciding how you can best come to their aid.

Sales Managers must lead!

Focus on a simple fact: How you got the job really doesn't matter—what matters is what you do with the assignment starting day one! It begins with leadership, sales teams follow leaders—resumes notwithstanding!

TEST YOUR KNOWLEDGE

1. What is the essential difference between sales and sales management?

   ....

2. When you work through other people, you share in and become responsible for their accomplishments and failings.   True/False

3. Entry-level sales management assignments are often restricted in scope and responsibility.   True/False

4. Top sales representatives earn more than most sales managers.   True/False

5. "It is always better to inherit a successful sales team!" Explain why this statement is not always correct.

   ....

6. List five of the steps from The Fast Start Plan.

   ...., ...

   ...., ...

   ....

7. Nothing will tell you more about the skills each salesperson possesses than watching them sell.   True/False

8. Sales managers lacking sales experience should:
   ❏ Avoid the lack of experience issue.
   ❏ Focus on big picture challenges and leave assisting the salespeople to others.
   ❏ All of the above.
   ❏ None of the above.

9. New sales managers should move quickly to remove salespeople who have been obvious performance failures.   True/False

10. The challenge of inheriting a failing team is:
    ❏ A limited window of time.
    ❏ The lack of organizational cooperation you will receive.
    ❏ Salespeople who will be too busy to listen.
    ❏ The problem may be greater than just a sales issue.

209

PART III

THE TRUTH ABOUT MANAGING

CHAPTER 18

Salespeople Are — Salespeople!

Managing salespeople is much like herding cats!
They are fiercely independent, smart, energetic,
occasionally attentive, and every so often—obedient.

The very qualities that make salespeople successful often conspire to make them a challenge to manage. You can expect to be questioned, doubted, tested, argued with and if you do your job correctly—respected and followed.

The experience of working in sales is valuable to aspiring managers because it gives you the opportunity to grasp the sales fraternity and its culture, while observing first hand how other people approach managing a sales team. You will learn by watching and personally experiencing managers who succeed and fail.

Sales and sales management are unique business occupations for one very specific reason—the results! There is little room for spin, explanation or excuses. The results are ever present, clearly defined and very public. I have listened to salespeople attempt to explain away poor performance more times then I care to recall. At best, the explanations might buy a temporary reprieve; but in the end, measurable results carry the day.

The uniqueness of the assignment drives the challenge of managing in this environment. Sales managers are held accountable for the results their sales team achieves. Try as you may as a sales manager, it's difficult to personally do the job of one single sales representative, let alone five, ten or more. Requiring or expecting a team to manage itself will not get you success, nor will demanding everything be done exactly as you prescribe. Professionals come to understand the only path to success is to lead your followers!

Sales is not for the faint of heart or those who are driven by the need to find a safe and inconspicuous job. Yet, the followers are all unique. I describe them as brilliant, energetic, skilled, and focused, as well as ordinary, flawed and occasionally incompetent! Most just want to make plan, others are driven beyond all else to extraordinary achievements. Salespeople will follow managers they respect and those who can help them succeed. Their loyalty can be earned and unfortunately lost! Being both outspoken and opinionated often comes with the sales personality. Salespeople will join and leave your team—making recruiting, training and terminating continuous managerial responsibilities.

Are they mercenaries or real team members? The answer is both! Many will protect their own interests and yours if it is to their advantage. They will sell because it's what they were hired to do and are commissioned to perform. Being in sales without selling anything is not very rewarding. Salespeople will behave as mercenaries if they are treated as such. When you pressure them to perform, they will respond by pressuring you to lead. If you can't or will not clear their path to success, they will conclude your interests and theirs are not aligned. These same sales professionals will demand that you get out of the way or they will express displeasure loud and clear. "If you can't help me succeed—that's bad. But I will not allow you to prevent me from succeeding!"

Experienced sales practitioners understand they are personally accountable for results. What is also understood is sales managers who prevent success are not to be respected or tolerated! Rebellions are not unusual and frequently result in managerial changes. The personalities that accept the risks of a sales career will not easily stomach inept management. Many have experienced enough managerial incompetence to quickly form opinions and act. Business owners and executive managers don't need to be reminded of the value cohesive sales teams provide.

Many sales representatives realize every year, quarter, or month is a new deal. They work in the present with an eye to the future of their current employer. Working in sales teaches you that changing market fortunes are inevitable. Salespeople enjoy being part of companies that are sales friendly. These enterprises are well-managed, offer top compensation plans and good products. The idea of working at troubled entities is not as appealing. The patience of professional sales representatives is often frustratingly short. Why? Time is money and if they can't earn commissions, time's a-wasting! Top performers, good salespeople and experienced practitioners—the core performers on most teams—will never have difficulty finding their next job. You need them far more than they need you ...a fact your salespeople fully appreciate!

Are the top performers all prima donnas? No! Some can be humble and decent, while others are true divas. It never concerned me if a top performer was difficult; what did concern me were marginal performers with oversized egos. The bottom line for salespeople is simple—deliver! That simple act forgives a lot of faults, personality quirks and mistakes. I can assure you, the herding of cats analogy will not be lost on sales managers. Leaders learn how to push, pull, praise and discipline salespeople all the while supporting their quest to excel.

Sales managers have to earn respect rather than expect it to come from a

215

position or title. This concept can be difficult for first-time managers to grasp, especially ex-prima donnas! The audience you are managing is not docile, timid, or without ego and confidence. They are used to asking prospects and customers difficult questions. Salesmen and saleswomen will challenge authority figures with opinions and criticism. It always amazed me how some salespeople knew more than everyone associated with the business, regardless of the topic! You will experience the same amazement.

Salespeople ultimately reflect the competence of their managers. Great performances are orchestrated by competent managers, poor results point to a manager who has struggled. The salespeople on your team are not your friends, nor the enemy—they are your primary constituency—the people you are responsible for leading to achievements beyond their own reach and...whose success will become your own legacy.

Sales managers who embody leadership, communication, motivation and coaching, among so many other skills, are best qualified to herd the cats!

CHAPTER 19

What's Your Personal Contribution?

Leaders roll up their sleeves and take on tasks they can impact by leveraging the weight of their title, office or expertise.

Every sales manager has four constituencies that they need to serve and manage. It's also important to carve out a role in the on-going challenges a sales team confronts. Your role may change each month, quarter or year, but your team should know you will make a personal contribution to their success.

Isn't being in charge a role? It certainly is! Your team expects you to lead, coach, teach and manage. What they will truly appreciate is your leading by undertaking specific difficult tasks which you have a unique ability to effect positively:

"I'm personally available to call on any prospect when a salesperson is facing a difficult competitive contest and I'll stay involved as long as they ask!"

"I will work the customer base to find this team several new reference accounts."

"This presentation is so important, I will be in attendance."

"I am the sales contact point with a particularly uncooperative engineering executive who is making our job difficult."

Explicit contributions like these are ones you will embrace personally to make everyone more successful!

Sales managers can make calls, deliver important messages, assure prospects, calm customers and solve issues that salespeople struggle to perform. I spent years as a successful salesperson, but I still needed a sales manager who could do things, go places and issue promises that were beyond my reach. Prospects often want a sales manager to tell them, "My company will do this for you!" Executive buyers respond more quickly to a VP of Sales asking for a meeting than they do to calls from a sales representative. Sales managers have a unique contribution they alone can deliver.

I worked for managers who were a very important part of my sales team. They were ready and able to bring the weight of authority to any deal where I requested help. Any constituency was fair game for assistance! They sometimes joked about role reversal, because they always made themselves available to help me win business.

I also labored for managers who were in charge—of being in charge! They were generally absent and added little or no value to my individual efforts. I held them in generally low regard and succeeded in spite of their presence. Their going-away parties were gala events!

When salespeople speak about sales managers who add value, what they really mean is their manager leads by doing tasks that they alone are uniquely qualified to perform. These are managers who go out of their way to be certain sales representatives get every edge possible in the search for new customers.

When managers roll-up their sleeves, they also exemplify leadership by example. Salespeople watch their managers perform the task and realize they are willing to do what has been asked of them—learning occurs, respect builds. Want to help someone make better calls? Close orders? Let them watch you perform. Make cold calls or do presentations with representatives who aren't comfortable or particularly good at the task. Teach by example!

Sales managers sometimes are fearful the effort they make will fail or turn out less than satisfactory. "My salespeople will see me falling short!" The truth is you will fail at times and you should expect it. I always volunteered to help, but I never gave anyone a 100% guarantee of my success. None of us who have worked as sales executives can guarantee anything but diligence, focus and effort. Even the best-laid plans, flawlessly executed sometimes don't work! As a sales rep once told me, "You did great, we lost, but I learned a lot. And if you couldn't win the deal, then I surely wouldn't have either!"

Always remind sales practitioners: "If I can do this, surely you can learn to do this as well...if not better!"

CHAPTER 20

The Assignment Is Temporary... The Results Aren't!

Entry-level sales management positions are temporary by nature and serve as the intersection of innumerable career choices. The endeavor is a difficult test from which incumbents are promoted to greater responsibilities in the sales arena, or given other key missions in an enterprise. The executives watching the performance of first time sales managers understand that the position requires leadership, team building, customer-facing skills and the ability to deliver measurable results from a group of individual contributors. It's a big challenge which speaks volumes about the leadership skills you possess!

The assignments last from 18 to 36 months—just enough time to demonstrate competence and grow in professional standing, however, the results of your effort will be with you for years to come. You will either enjoy and leverage a record of achievement or continue to explain the failure. What career options likely lay ahead for the best performers? At least five attractive directions are available for those who have succeeded in sales management.

A Return to sales

Some sales managers will decide to return to being individual sales contributors. They want to stay in sales but conclude that "moving up the organization wasn't really a step up." A return to top-tier compensation plans and the relief of managing no one other than themselves can often present a powerful tug! Some of the most competent and successful people I have known mastered sales management and then returned to sales.

Management

Sales managers become managers of a wide assortment of business functions. The experience of supervising a revenue plan establishes their credentials in marketing, product management, customer service, brand management, and general management assignments. The existence of a successful sales management role, early in a career, pays dividends years later when you are competing for senior managerial positions.

Vice President of Sales

The managers who thrive as entry-level sales managers often decide to work towards becoming senior sales management executives. The executive responsible for a business's top line revenue is influential and powerful. The Vice President of Sales sets sales strategy, drives budgets and manages a revenue stream. The job may be an end in itself or a stepping-stone to owning or managing the full business enterprise.

Executive Management

The ranks of executive management are heavily populated with ex-sales executives. Why? A business rises and falls, first and foremost, on its ability to create and sustain customers—a reality sales executives are uniquely prepared to manage.

A CEO may or may not be a sales executive, however, you will find one or more executives on the executive management team with significant sales expertise.

Entrepreneurship

Yes, a number of sales managers start their own businesses. Once you understand how to create and manage revenue, the opportunity to own a business becomes very tempting, "I did it for someone else—I can do it this time for myself!"

There is a reason many sales managers who fail in their initial assignment continue to try to succeed! They come to appreciate the multitude of outstanding career options top managers can choose and how difficult it can be to explain a disappointing performance.

Select your first sales management assignment carefully. Make certain you work tirelessly to learn and polish the skills the assignment demands, lead your sales team to its goals, and then decide what your next career step will be!

CHAPTER 21

Failure — Why It Happens

Sales managers fail! They fail initially and at various points in their career, some will fail far more often then they succeed. Our discussion is going to focus on failures which are within the officeholder's ability to correct, failure that belongs on your shoulders—because it could have been avoided!

The defeats that result from choosing to work for floundering employers, becoming embroiled in political turf wars, or basic product catastrophes are real, but beyond the scope of this chapter.

The "I'm the boss" disconnect

On the way back from lunch, the CEO I was interviewing with broke a moment of silence, "I want you to be part of our company but that's not going to happen, is it?"

"I don't think we have a real good fit. You're not ready to surrender control of the business and I am not looking for another VP of Sales position."

He shook his head in agreement, "Next flight isn't until later this evening. Would you do me a favor and sit with one of my sales directors?"

"Sure, tell me what you want accomplished."

"Joe was a sales rep at our company. He was competent but not a star performer, a real bulldog. He wore me down, kept asking to be a sales manager. I needed one and I finally agreed." The tone of his voice betrayed his disappointment.

"Not worked very well?"

"Right...see what you think the problem is."

Joe sat stiffly at his desk, meeting with me was not on his list of must-do's. "Are you the new VP of Sales?"

"Nope, good company, but not a good fit for me."

"The boss said I should talk with you about sales management. So talk."

"Actually, Joe, I was interested in learning how you approach being a sales manager."

He glared at me as if this was really trying his patience, "My approach?"

"Yes, your approach."

"Managing a sales team is a cross between being a prison warden and a zookeeper. I don't tolerate much nonsense, I expect them to do their jobs—plain and simple."

"So, how have the results been?"

"Not very good, but you already know that, don't you?" His anger and hostility were close to alarming.

"Joe, I'm not here to fight with you. You're much too big and I'm much too old! Your boss asked me for a favor, so here I am! I have to tell you, the zookeeper comments are difficult to understand."

His body language was still very tense, "The salespeople I have are immature, mischievous and always cutting corners. They are in it for themselves...they do anything to get what they want. My job is to keep them in line and make sure they follow the rules. I always did my job professionally, I don't think asking them to do the same is so unreasonable."

"Do they think you're unreasonable?"

"I'm the boss, I really don't care what they think!"

"Joe, we both know how poor your numbers look. Fair or not, something has to change. What's the change going to be?"

He stared at me with a look of disbelief. "They have to start doing things my way or I start firing anyone who isn't at plan!"

"Your boss just finished telling me how difficult it is to find salespeople. Who's going to replace the ones you fire? Is anyone on your team at plan?"

"Two of the eight are at plan. Am I...Are you trying to tell me something?"

"Joe, I've been in sales and sales management long enough to know that when you are at 40% of plan, something will change."

The look on his face changed, "I need more time to work through this, 10 months isn't enough time! I'll get these darn people turned around!"

I got up, handed him a business card and offered him this advice: "Sales managers are in charge of sales teams—but just being appointed 'boss' will not get the job done!" Focus on making each person on the team successful by communicating, coaching, and teaching. Their success is your success, their failure's yours! Leaders inspire followers and work to grow the sales skills of each team member. They listen and respond to challenges. Leadership goes far beyond a philosophy of discipline or reminding people you're in charge!

Avoiding leadership

"It's really difficult to follow someone who can't lead!" Sales managers often avoid leadership because they don't know how to lead, others try but stumble and some are just not interested. The end result is unfortunately the same—followers who fend for themselves or turn off and walk away— organizational drift and then failure! I have worked for and with enough sales managers to know this progression to failure is quite predictable and avoidable.

Leadership fortunately is a skill which can be both learned and enhanced. If you don't know how to lead or are struggling as a leader, you have an opportunity to learn, grow and succeed. The progress you make will reflect how hard you work at learning and your personal persistence. If you are not interested in leading, you shouldn't accept a sales management position!

Executive managers and your followers don't expect perfect leadership, especially from early career sales managers, but what they do expect is your best efforts and the ability to learn from inevitable mistakes. Leaders understand they will spend a full career making leadership errors and learning!

The sales management assignment is for most incumbents the first test of leadership skills. In Part I, we discussed many of the skills which underpin and define leadership—the ability to communicate, motivate, coach and hold salespeople accountable. Perhaps none of these skills is more fundamental than the act of setting goals.

The goals you set tell your team where it is going! For most sales managers the most basic of all goals is the revenue plan. Focus your team and yourself on the revenue plan and you will have taken the first concrete step to leadership. Remember—a Goal leads to Actions and Actions produce measurable Results! The same concept top sales professionals understand and embrace works for sales managers learning to lead.

Tell each salesperson the revenue plan is the goal—and you have started to communicate! Once the team knows where you are taking them, they will ask: "How will we get there? What about this or that?" This communication leads to more discussion, decisions, plans and leadership!

Ignoring sales skills

Sales managers need selling skills and expertise. The challenge is to migrate from primarily doing selling work to teaching and assisting others as they sell. It's a fatal mistake to think a sales manager can somehow divorce or separate himself from selling. You will continue to sell—or you will fail! Please, don't ever take a sales management position in an attempt to get out of sales!

The selling responsibility expands because you manage strategy, set policy, develop sales methodologies and clear the path to success—not for yourself, but for a team of salespeople. You need to know how to prospect, make introductory calls, create value propositions, present proposals, handle objections and close business. The sales challenges you face will increase because you are responsible for every sales representative on your team, and for the problems they encounter.

Is your managerial assignment at a different business, in a new market, or driven by a unique sales model? If it is, you will have to adapt your sales skills to this new environment. The relearning process can be difficult and time consuming. How quickly and effectively you embrace a new sales model will be important to a fast personal start. Trust me on this, your sales team will grow impatient hearing advice that doesn't pertain to their sales environment! Sales managers who lack sales experience have to work extra hard to get up-to-speed.

Most managers will effect change in their selling organization. They will refine or improve a sales methodology, revise forecasting, change discount policies, make personnel changes—all things which require you to select alternatives and make decisions. The sales experience you bring to the assignment will help you to make smart choices.

The best sales managers are those who have a depth of sales knowledge, broad experience, a passion for the profession, and are quick learners!

Mishandling constituencies

Sales managers who neglect one or several of their key audiences fail.

I have watched managers ignore or antagonize the business's customers and their concerns. I have listened to colleagues bitterly complain about sales managers who built barriers and generated conflict within a business. Executive managers were dismayed because they felt sales managers kept them in the dark and away from the sales team. Finally, sales representatives feel mishandled when they cannot find or get any assistance from their manager. Each mistake was serious!

The reason sales management assignments are so difficult is that you are required to engage and please each audience. Most managers have one, maybe two audiences to serve, but sales managers are held accountable by every internal and external constituency for almost everything! It's why those who can succeed are deemed very valuable.

Sales managers are told to fix customer problems, sell around product issues, deliver sales revenue plans, execute marketing programs—the list goes on and on.

I can recall an argument I had with my boss's boss who was angry I had not assigned enough sales representatives to persuade our customers to attend a users' conference. Fighting my annoyance, I chided him, "You want me to shutdown the sales efforts for this quarter with two weeks to go and work on the users' conference? That's what you are ordering me to do? I am sorry, but despite your advice, the users' conference has to wait—the quarter is first priority!"

Taking responsibility for your decisions is part and parcel of being a sales manager. The pressure to perform and serve many masters is real and unrelenting.

230

The demands are well-intentioned but never-ending! Incidentally, weeks after the conference was over, the same executive confided to me, "I'm glad you refused my advice about the users' conference. The quarter was far more crucial!"

I have learned that you can't please each audience all the time. Criticism and second guessing come with the territory. What you can't do is ignore, antagonize and debase—unless you want to fail!

What each constituency deserves is open and honest dialog and a prompt response, even if the answer is no more than, "I'm still thinking about your request!" When you have to say "No," take a few minutes to explain your reasoning and then move to the next issue. Candor goes a long way to reminding everybody you are sincerely trying your best and being sensitive to their needs. Sometimes the audiences just want you to acknowledge they are important and their comments are valuable!

I also learned and you will too—the sales team and your revenue plan are first among equals—from there all other good things follow!

A lack of passion
A passion for sales, the salesforce, revenue goals and the managerial assignment will carry you through the inevitable challenges that cause others to lose hope and focus. Leaders set the tone for a sales team. A salesforce needs to witness a positive attitude, commitment, enthusiasm and energy from its leader—consistently. Followers are devastated by managers who give up the crusade to succeed. Even on your worst days your team should see and feel the passion that you have for the assignment—nothing less will suffice!

Sales managers who lack passion for their assignment are truly doomed! Each constituency expects and demands passion. If they sense it's missing, alarms will sound across the entire organization. Why? Sales management is critically important to the business and all its employees. Whenever a manager struggles with their morale, everyone will assume the worst—we are failing! The executives of a business will not permit a manager to demoralize the sales team, by exhibiting a lack of passion!

The best sales managers
cultivate and grow the skills
and careers of each salesperson
and colleague they touch.

They fertilize, prune and weed!
The businesses they work at thrive.
Customers sprout and multiply.

Gardeners!

TEST YOUR KNOWLEDGE

1. The very qualities that make salespeople successful often conspire to make them a challenge to manage.   True/False

2. Are salespeople mercenaries or real team members?
   - ❏ Mercenaries
   - ❏ Team members
   - ❏ Both
   - ❏ Neither

3. Sales representatives often conclude that sales managers who prevent success are not to be respected or tolerated!   True/False

4. Sales managers have to earn respect rather then expect it to come from a position or title.   True/False

5. Leaders roll up their sleeves and take on tasks they can impact by leveraging the weight of their title, office or expertise.   True/False

6. Most entry-level sales management assignments are positions that represent the final stop in a career plan.   True/False

7. List five career options successful first-time sales managers can

   choose to pursue: _____, _____,

   _____, _____ and _____.

8. Common reasons first-time sales managers fail include:
   - ❏ The "I'm the boss" disconnect.
   - ❏ Avoiding leadership.
   - ❏ Forgetting sales skills still matter.
   - ❏ All the above.

9. Sales managers who lack passion for their assignment are truly doomed!   True/False

10. Explain the analogy between Gardeners and Sales Managers.

_____

_____

APPENDIX A

Index of Illustrations

Goal-Action-Result Continuum	32
Managerial Control of the Sales Environment	56
The Business Sales Methodology	64
Goal-Action-Result Steps of The Business Sales Methodology	66-67
The Steps To Managing A Key Account	88-89
Definition of Upside/Commit Accounts	94
Steps to Forecasting Upside Accounts	99
Definition of Upside/Commit Accounts	101
The Sales Pipeline	104
Effective Forecasting Workbook	113-122
A Top Performer	134
The 10 Personal Skills of Top Performers	137
Sales Compensation Plan	169
The Four Constituencies	182
The Fast Start Plan	198
Five Reasons for Failure	226
The Four Constituencies	230
Gardeners	233

APPENDIX B

Index of Forms

The Steps To Managing A Key Account   88

Effective Forecasting Workbook   113

    Prospect Forecast   115

    Sales Representative Forecast   116

    Consolidated Forecast   117

    Sales Representative Pipeline   118

    Consolidated Pipeline   119

    Lost Prospect Analysis   120

    Sales Compensation Plan   121

    Upside/Commit Definitions   122

APPENDIX C

Illustrations:
The Steps To Managing A Key Account

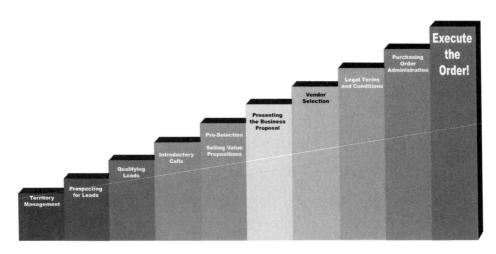

The Business Sales Methodology

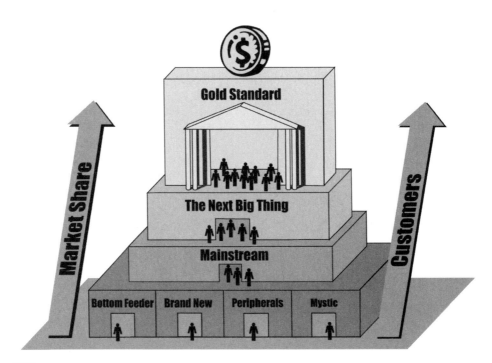

THE
"Cs"
CEO - CFO

EXECUTIVE
BUYERS
EVP - SVP - Group VP

Business Executives with Budget
THE CIO
Technologist Who Recommends

THE RECOMMENDERS
Vice Presidents or Directors
Department - Product - Functional Managers

THE EVALUATORS
Consultants - Project Managers - Technical Specialists
Coaches   Gatekeepers

COMPETITOR'S

Who specifically are the competitors?

When do you compete?

What is their business history?

Who are the principals and key employees?

Where are their locations?

What business strategy and goals are they pursuing?

How strong is their financial performance?

Who are their most important customers?

How do they service and support customers?

What type of reputation do they have with customers and suppliers?

How do they perform essential marketing and promotion activities?

RESUME

How do they sell their products? What are the channels to market?

....

What are their products?

- Build an overview statement

....

- Analyze each product's strengths/weaknesses

....

- Pricing

....

- Terms and conditions

....

- Inventory levels

....

- Partners and suppliers

....

What specific opportunities have they won at your expense?

....

Why do they win business?

....

Which competitive profile do they fit?

....

INDEX

A
Account management, 82-89, 102, 238-241
Agendas, 49, 59, 172-175

B
Budgets, 123-131
Business Sales Methodology, 64, 66-67, 87-89, 97, 99, 110, 238

C
Chief motivation officer, 40-41, 173
Coaching, 47-52, 70
Commissions, 160-165, 169
Communication skills, 15-28, 32-34, 48, 83, 174, 201
Competitor's Profile, 87, 89, 238
Competitor's Resume, 87, 89, 240-241
Consolidated Forecast, 117
Consolidated Pipeline, 119
Constituencies, 26, 181-184, 190, 216, 218, 230
Counter-offers, 150-152

D
Dispute resolution, 59

E
Employment practices, 57, 146-147, 165
Entrepreneurship, 12, 223
Ethics, 48, 57
External sales environment, 63-64
Evaluating, 133-157

F
Fast Start Plan, 193, 198
First Assignments, 195-203, 222
Five Reasons for Failure, 225-231
Forecasts, 91-122, 202
Forecasting Workbook, 113-122
Four Constituencies, 181-184, 218, 230
Four Simple Rules of Forecasting, 98-101

G

Gardener, 14, 178, 232
Goals, 12, 28, 31-37, 50, 66-67, 106, 201, 228
Goal-Action-Result Continuum, 16, 28, 32, 66-67, 89, 106, 229
Grievance resolution, 59

I

Internal sales environment, 56-63
Interview process, 201

K

Key Account Plan, 88-89, 238-241

L

Leadership, 15-17, 50, 58, 83, 172-174, 200, 208, 214, 218, 228, 231
Listening skills, 16-25, 201
Lost Prospect Analysis, 104, 120

M

Managing failing teams, 196-198
Managing successful teams, 196-197
Managing the metrics, 60, 65, 69-72
Measurements, 69-74
      activity-related, 70
      prospect feedback, 70, 71
      transformational, 70, 71
Messages, 21-25, 64, 104, 173, 174
Motivation, 39-44, 50, 172, 201, 228

O

Objection handling, 23, 99

P

Performance, 59, 60, 70, 93, 96, 202
Personal contributions, 217-219
Pipeline, 103-106
Pre-selection selling, 66-67, 99-103, 110
Prospect Forecast, 115

Q

Qualifying, 66-67, 103, 104, 142, 207
Quotas, 33, 160-165, 169

R

Recruiting, 134-138, 141-144, 156, 202, 208, 214
Resignations, 149-151
Revenue plans, 33, 82, 98, 124, 128, 160-165, 192-193, 230-231

S

Sales administration, 59
Sales compensation, 96, 97, 206, 107, 159-170
Sales Compensation Plan, 121, 169
Sales Management Assignments, 187-208, 228, 230
Sales meetings, 171-175
Sales Pipeline, 103, 104
Sales Representative Forecast, 116
Sales Representative Pipeline, 118
Sales skills, 64, 229
Selling environment, 55-68, 70, 71, 191, 196
Selling time, 56, 57, 64, 76, 82
Steps To Managing A Key Account, 88-89, 238-241

T

Tactical plans, 33, 34
Terminations, 146, 147, 202, 214
Territory management, 32, 66, 67, 163, 201
Test Your Knowledge, 29, 38, 45, 53, 68, 74, 79, 90, 112, 132, 157, 170, 180, 185, 209, 234
The Selling Pyramid, 67, 87-88, 115, 239
The 10 Skills of Top Performers, 137
Top Performers, 76, 134-138, 215
Training, 145, 146, 172, 214
Transition, 190-193

U

Upside/Commit Accounts, 94, 99-102, 122

V

Value of Accounts, 102-104
Value proposition, 104, 120, 122

About The Author

Tom knows first hand the dedication and exceptional efforts it takes to achieve business success. His 25 years of global experience creates a valuable perspective of the challenges faced by sales and marketing practitioners in today's hyper-competitive markets.

He shares with his readers the necessary skills to achieve sustainable success and offers a unique methodical approach to surmounting business challenges.

Butler holds a BBA from St. Bonaventure University and is a graduate of The Stonier School.

He resides with his family in Vero Beach, Florida.

Business Skills...
Self-Help for Careers!

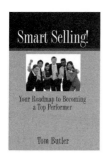

Smart Selling!

Learn both fundamental selling skills and a repeatable customer-oriented selling methodology you can put to work now! We'll teach you what to do, how to do it, and why it's important! Discover what top sales professionals understand about achieving sustainable success. The enhanced 2006 edition is currently used in college level professional selling courses.

Page Count: 208 • Size: 7"x 10" • ISBN 0-9772169-0-X • Paperback $19.99

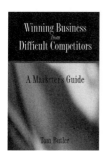

Winning Business from Difficult Competitors

The competition for new and existing customers has never been more intense or of greater importance. Ultimate success for each marketer, salesperson, and business owner comes from winning new business from the competition. We explore the detailed profiles of seven types of adversaries. Learn what attracts potential customers to each profile and how to prevail.

Page Count: 192 • Size 7"x 10" • ISBN 0-9772169-1-8 • Paperback $19.99

Profitable Trade Show Exhibiting

What are the latest trends in today's trade shows? Smart exhibitors are demanding measurable results that impact their bottom line. They want sales and qualified leads! This new conviction extends from basic consumer-oriented shows to large business-to-business events. Positively impact your sales and profits through simple, clear and concise actions.

Page Count: 160 • Size 5.5"x 8.5" • ISBN 0-9718039-8-6 • Paperback $14.99

The Publisher: Business Skills Press

Our business mission and commitment is to provide books for students, entrepreneurs and aspiring business people. The titles teach, enhance and refresh the skills required for successful careers. Author lectures and Instructor PowerPoints are available.

Information and Orders • Call: 206-794-3473
Visit: www.BusinessSkillsPress.com
Write: P.O. Box 690656, Vero Beach, Florida 32969